# *How to Pass*

## NATIONAL 5

# German

Kirsten Herbst-Gray

HODDER
GIBSON
AN HACHETTE UK COMPANY

The Publishers would like to thank the following for permission to reproduce copyright material:

**Acknowledgements**

The SQA marking grids for the Writing Course Assessment (pp. 55–57) and the Talking Course Assessment (pp. 61–63) are reproduced by kind permission Copyright © Scottish Qualifications Authority.

All worked examples and solutions within this title were devised by the author.

Every effort has been made to trace all copyright holders, but if any have been inadvertently overlooked the Publishers will be pleased to make the necessary arrangements at the first opportunity.

Although every effort has been made to ensure that website addresses are correct at time of going to press, Hodder Gibson cannot be held responsible for the content of any website mentioned in this book. It is sometimes possible to find a relocated web page by typing in the address of the home page for a website in the URL window of your browser.

Hachette Livre UK's policy is to use papers that are natural, renewable and recyclable products and made from wood grown in sustainable forests. The logging and manufacturing processes are expected to conform to the environmental regulations of the country of origin.

Orders: please contact Bookpoint Ltd, 130 Park Drive, Abingdon, Oxon OX14 4SE. Telephone: (44) 01235 827720. Fax: (44) 01235 400454 Lines are open 9.00–5.00, Monday to Saturday, with a 24-hour message answering service. Visit our website at www.hoddereducation.co.uk. Hodder Gibson can be contacted direct on: Tel: 0141 848 1609; Fax: 0141 889 6315; email: hoddergibson@hodder.co.uk

© Kirsten Herbst-Gray 2015

First published in 2015 by
Hodder Gibson, an imprint of Hodder Education,
An Hachette UK Company,
2a Christie Street
Paisley PA1 1NB

Impression number    5    4    3    2    1

Year    2019    2018    2017    2016    2015

Cover photo © Zarya Maxim — Fotolia.com
Illustrations by Barking Dog Art Design and Illustration
Typeset in Cronos Pro Light 13/15pt by Aptara, Inc.
Printed in Spain
A catalogue record for this title is available from the British Library
ISBN: 978 1 471 84321 1

# Contents

# Introduction

*Hallo und Guten Tag!*

Are you in S4 or S5 and keen to get ready for your National 5 German exam? Great – this book is just right for you. It will help you to understand the National 5 German standard of performance, the course contents, its units and unit assessments and – last but not least – will give you plenty of useful information about the National 5 German course assessment together with lots of practice material.

German is easier than you think – you have nothing to worry about.

*Los geht's! Let's start.*

# What you should know about German

Before you read more about National 5 German, you should take a few minutes to look at some of the similarities between English and German. These will help you to recognise German words and you won't need to learn so much vocabulary!

English and German are both members of the same language family – the Germanic language family. The majority of everyday words in the English language are of Germanic origin and modern German and English vocabulary have a lot in common. Your German teacher will call these words 'cognates' or 'near-cognates'.

**Remember**

Try to increase your awareness of the relationship between the English language and the German language. It will make learning German so much easier and will give you more confidence in understanding and using the language.

This is a very small selection of cognates and near-cognates.

| **English and German nouns** | | **English and German verbs** | | **English and German adjectives** | |
|---|---|---|---|---|---|
| house | *das Haus* | to help | *helfen* | good | *gut* |
| garden | *der Garten* | to sing | *singen* | better | *besser* |
| bus | *der Bus* | to drink | *trinken* | best | *(am) besten* |
| school | *die Schule* | to park | *parken* | fantastic | *fantastisch* |
| family | *die Familie* | to swim | *schwimmen* | friendly | *freundlich* |
| sun | *die Sonne* | to send | *senden* | unfriendly | *unfreundlich* |
| ship | *das Schiff* | to begin | *beginnen* | warm | *warm* |
| mouse | *die Maus* | to sink | *sinken* | open | *offen* |

This is a very small selection of common words in English and German. Your German teacher will call these words 'internationalisms' as they are pretty much the same in a number of languages.

| | | | | | |
|---|---|---|---|---|---|
| abstract | *abstrakt* | ideal | *ideal* | qualification | *die Qualifikation* |
| banana | *die Banane* | yoghurt | *der Joghurt* | restaurant | *das Restaurant* |
| computer | *der Computer* | coffee | *der Kaffee* | supermarket | *der Supermarkt* |
| doctor | *der Doktor* | list | *die Liste* | taxi | *das Taxi* |
| extreme | *extrem* | market | *der Markt* | university | *die Universität* |
| fair | *fair* | normal | *normal* | virus | *der Virus* |
| guitar | *die Gitarre* | orchestra | *das Orchester* | centre | *das Zentrum* |
| hobby | *das Hobby* | perfect | *perfekt* | | |

# What you should know about the National 5 German Course

National 5 German has been designed to support you in achieving some level of proficiency in the language so that you will be able to read, listen, talk and write in German on topics and sub-topics in four different contexts – society, learning, employability and culture.

*Remember*

Society – Learning – Employability – Culture = SLEC

*Check this out*

Here is an overview of the four contexts, their topics and sub-topics.

| Society | Family and friends | Saying how you get on with family members and who has influenced you in your life |
| --- | --- | --- |
| | | Arguments |
| | | Ideal parents |
| | | Different types of friends |
| | | Peer pressure |
| | Lifestyle | Lifestyle-related illnesses |
| | | Advantages and disadvantages of healthy/unhealthy lifestyle |
| | Media | Impact of TV reality shows |
| | | Advantages/disadvantages of new technology, e.g., internet, mobile phones |
| | Global languages | Language-learning and relevance |
| | Citizenship | Description of local area as a tourist centre |
| | | Comparison of town and country life |
| | | Being environmentally friendly in the home |
| Learning | Learning in context | Talk about what learning activities you like/dislike in different subjects |
| | | Preparing for exams |
| | Education | Comparing education systems |
| | | Improving own education system |
| | | Learner responsibilities |

$\Rightarrow$

| Employability | Jobs | Part-time jobs and studying |
| --- | --- | --- |
| | | Qualities for present/future jobs/future plans |
| | Work and CVs | Planning, reporting back on work experience |
| | | Reviewing achievements/ambitions |
| Culture | Planning a trip | Importance of travel and learning a foreign language |
| | | Describing your best holiday/trip/attitudes to travel |
| | Other countries | Aspects of other countries including educational, social, historical, political aspects |
| | Celebrating a special event | Comparing special occasions/traditions/celebrations/events in German-speaking countries |
| | | Importance of customs/traditions |
| | Literature of German-speaking countries | Literary fiction, e.g. short stories — understanding and analysis |
| | Film and television | Studying films in German |
| | | Studying television in German-speaking countries |

National 5 German gives your German teacher the opportunity to decide how to further develop the topics and sub-topics. This will be important for the unit assessments you have to pass. Your teacher will be able to assess you in different ways, using different approaches.

The course consists of two units: **Understanding Language** and **Using Language**.

# Unit 1: Understanding Language

This unit focuses on the development of reading and listening skills in German. Throughout the course, your German teacher will help you to read and listen to more complex German texts and extract straightforward as well as more detailed information. Your teacher will also help you to understand the overall purpose of the text.

Your teacher will assess you when you are ready. This could be done naturally as part of class work or it could be done in a more formal way. **There are no deadlines for passing unit assessments. They are not graded but are simply marked as pass/fail.** You just need to show that you are able to cope with a National 5 Reading or Listening text by understanding the overall purpose and being able to extract some details from the text. Easy!

## Check this out (!)

### What is 'overall purpose'?

Whenever you read a text (or listen to a text) in any language, you should be aware that texts are produced for a reason and/or a certain audience. This could be to advertise a product, to promote a place of interest, to express concern about a situation, to invite somebody to an event, to give an opinion about a matter – to name but a few. This should sound familiar to you from your English classes.

## Unit 2: Using Language

This unit focuses on the development of talking and writing skills in German. Your teacher might call them 'productive skills' because you 'produce' German as relevant to you.

Throughout the whole course, your German teacher will help you to develop your talking and writing skills in different ways. You may find that your teacher speaks a lot of German in class and asks students to read words, sentences and texts out loud. You may also find that your teacher asks your class to conduct short conversations on familiar topics in class or asks students questions in German on a certain item, picture or text. You should join in these activities whenever possible because they give you the opportunity to practise your language skills and become more confident. And do not worry about making mistakes – you will still be understood and nobody is perfect!

Your teacher will assess you when you are ready. This could be done naturally as part of class work or it could be done in a more formal way. **There are no deadlines for passing unit assessments. They are not graded but are simply marked as pass/fail.** You just need to show that you are able to 'produce' a written or spoken text which contains National 5 German features of language difficulties. Plenty of practice and a good portion of diligence will make you succeed!

# What you should know about the National 5 German Unit Assessment

## Reading

Your teacher might give you one or more texts for reading comprehension. The new approach to unit assessment allows your teacher to decide what types of comprehension questions are most suitable.

## Possible question types

### 1 True, false or not in the text

You are presented with statements on the text and have to decide whether they are true, false or whether the text does not contain any information on them.

### 2 Multiple choice

You are presented with more than one answer or statement and have to decide which answer or statement is correct. This is a popular question type for the 'overall purpose' question.

### 3 Gap filling

You are presented with a gap fill text and have to complete the text correctly. You might be provided with words to fill the gaps. Your teacher might ask you questions on the text after you have filled the gaps.

### 4 Completing a grid

You are presented with a grid and have to complete it with information from the text. This is a popular comprehension task if there is more than one reading text.

### 5 Questions on the text

These questions will be in English and you will have to answer in English. Unit assessment questions in Reading will be open and allow you flexibility in your answers. For example, if you understand additional information from the text, you will not be penalised if you give more details in your answer.

> ### Check this out ❗
>
> The unit assessment Reading is marked as pass or fail. There is no grade.
>
> Whatever questions you are given, try to understand the structure of the text by looking at each paragraph and thinking about its main point(s).
>
> You are allowed to use a dictionary – so brush up on your dictionary skills and, even better, get your own dictionary. It will be your best friend in assessment situations.

# Listening 🔊

Your teacher might present you with a monologue (one speaker) or a dialogue (two speakers) to listen to in German. You will be allowed to listen to the passage a number of times. The new approach to unit assessment allows your teacher to decide what types of comprehension questions are most suitable. In many cases, the types of questions in Reading and Listening are very similar.

## Possible question types

### 1 True, false or not in the text

You are presented with statements on the listening passage and have to decide whether they are true, false or whether the passage does not contain any relevant information.

### 2 Multiple choice

You are presented with more than one answer or statement and have to decide which answer or statement is correct. This is a popular question type for the 'overall purpose' question.

### 3 Gap filling

You are presented with a gap fill sentence in English on the listening passage. You have to complete the gaps with the correct English words.

## 4 Completing a grid

You are presented with a grid and have to complete it with information from the listening passage.

## 5 Questions on the text

These questions will be in English and you will have to answer in English. Unit assessment questions in Listening will be open and allow you flexibility in your answers. For example, if you understand additional information from the listening passage, you will not be penalised if you give further details in your answer.

### Check this out

The unit assessment Listening is marked as pass or fail. There is no grade.

It is very important that you remember the similarities between English and German when it comes to listening. Relax and trust your intuition (gut feeling).

You will be allowed to listen to the passage a number of times. So it is not necessary to understand everything immediately.

Taking notes is a skill which is very important in listening comprehension. Make sure your notes reflect correctly what you have understood and that your English is of a good standard in order to convey meaning clearly.

# Talking 💬

Learning a modern language involves, first and foremost, using it for communication – asking and answering questions, expressing views and opinions, presenting a topic, to name but a few. Your teacher will ask you to read German out loud and to take part in German-only activities in class – either teacher-led or as pair work. This will help you to use spoken German and will give you confidence to speak the language as relevant to you.

Please do not underestimate the importance of grammar! It might be worthwhile to focus on some grammatical features as appropriate to your assessment. Grammar is not painful or difficult – it holds the words in a sentence together, and gives you the power and confidence to 'create' German.

There are no set rules for the unit assessment. Your teacher could ask you to do a presentation on a topic which you have just covered in class, or your talking assessment could be a brief conversation between you and your German teacher in class time as part of your coursework. You just need to show that you are able to use spoken German, including features of language as appropriate to National 5 standards.

> ## Check this out
>
> The Talking Unit Assessment is marked as pass or fail. There is no grade.
>
> You are in control of this assessment because your level of motivation and diligence will be important for your success. Always try to give information willingly – include an opinion and add any other detail you can think of. You can use your Talking Unit Assessment as part of your Talking Course Assessment which will save you time and reduce your workload later on in the year.

## Possible topics

Here are some examples of possible unit assessment topics to talk about in German. This list is not prescriptive; your German teacher might have included other sub-topics in the course.

### Society

*Meine Familie*
*Meine Freizeit*
*Meine Heimatstadt*

### Learning

*Meine Schule*
*Mein Lieblingsfach/Meine*
   *Lieblingsfächer*
*Deutsch lernen – warum?*

### Employability

*Mein Nebenjob*
*Mein Arbeitspraktikum*
*Ein Vorstellungsgespräch*

### Culture

*Meine letzten/nächsten*
   *Ferien*
*Schottland – Touristenland*
*Ein deutscher Film*

# Writing ✒

Text production is another form of communication in a language. You will be aware of this from your English classes. However, in German – and modern languages in general – writing brings together your knowledge of vocabulary, grammar and text structure. The unit assessment Writing can be part of your ongoing coursework or it can be done in a more formal way.

The National 5 unit assessment Writing is an **open–book assessment**. What does that mean?

- You can use a dictionary.
- You can use your coursework material.
- You can use any additional material which you might find relevant to solve the writing task your teacher gives you.

The focus of this assessment is to develop your writing skills holistically. What does that mean?

- Writing is a process which requires planning.
- Writing is a process which requires you to think ahead logically about the purpose and structure of your text.
- A written text needs to be checked over in order to ensure the highest possible level of accuracy.

So don't be surprised if your teacher provides you with a 'writing brief' which contains the writing task, some suggestions on how to tackle it and maybe even some references to books or websites you have used in class. Your teacher might even let you choose a writing topic of your personal preference! Make sure you show off your ability to write a text in German by including National 5 features of the language.

## Possible topics

Here are some examples of possible unit assessment topics to write about in German. This list is not prescriptive; your German teacher might have included other sub-topics in the course.

### Society

*Meine Familie und ich*
*Freunde und*
  *Freundschaft*
*Freizeit – meine Zeit!*

### Employability

*Ich über mich – meine Stärken*
  *und Schwächen*
*Mein tabellarischer Lebenslauf*
*Ein Bewerbungsschreiben*

### Learning

*Ein typischer Schultag in*
  *Schottland*
*Schuluniform in meiner*
  *Schule*
*Meine Schulfächer*

### Culture

*Meine besten Ferien*
*Mein Lieblingsbuch/*
  *Mein Lieblingsfilm*
*Eine Stadt in Deutschland:*
  *Hamburg, Berlin, München*

**Check this out**

The unit assessment Writing is marked as pass or fail. There is no grade.

You are in control of this assessment. Your success will depend on your motivation and diligence.

Always read the writing task carefully. Review your coursework material to find vocabulary and grammar points which could be helpful. Plan your writing and aim for a clear and logical structure of the text together with the highest possible level of accuracy.

Check your writing thoroughly before you hand it in for assessment.

Now it's time to practise some unit assessment tasks.

# Reading Unit Assessment

# Society

## Wie sollten Eltern sein?

In den meisten Fällen verstehen sich Eltern und Kinder sehr gut. Aber im Teenageralter kann es ab und zu Probleme geben. Vanessa und Ralph sagen ihre Meinung zum Thema Eltern.

## Vanessa (14 Jahre alt)

Meine Eltern haben einen richtigen Kontrolfimmel! Meine Mutter sagt mir jeden Abend, dass ich mich waschen und meine Zähne putzen muss – das weiß ich doch selbst! Außerdem wollen meine Eltern, dass ich jeden Abend um acht Uhr zu Hause bin, obwohl meine Freunde länger draußen bleiben dürfen. Aber am schlimmsten ist es, wenn mein Vater ständig auf meinem Handy anruft um zu fragen, wo ich bin und was ich mache. Das ist nicht nur mega peinlich sondern nervt mich total! Trotzdem liebe ich meine Eltern – sie sind immer für mich da und haben mich noch nie im Stich gelassen – außerdem helfen sie mir, wenn ich ein Problem habe.

## Raphael (15 Jahre alt)

Ich würde mir wünschen, dass mein Vater mehr Zeit für mich hat. Seit drei Monaten hat er mit versprochen, dass wir angeln gehen. Doch jedes Wochenende hat er keine Zeit, weil er sehr viel arbeitet und oft auf Dienstreise ist. Und dann ist er noch der Vorsitzende vom Tennisklub. Ich mache mir Sorgen, denn mein Vater ist oft gestresst und schlecht gelaunt wegen seiner Arbeit. Ich denke auch, dass er nicht genug schläft. Manchmal geht er erst nach Mitternacht ins Bett und um sieben Uhr ist er dann schon aus dem Haus. Meine Mutter ist immer da für mich – sie ist total toll. Ich bin mir nicht sicher, was ich ohne sie machen würde. Jedes Jahr freue ich mich auf die Sommerferien, weil wir dann alle zusammen wegfahren. Und dann wird aus meinem gestressten Vater ein echter Familienmensch!

## Questions

1 Vanessa says that her parents are very controlling. What examples does she give? State **at least three** things.
2 Vanessa says she loves her parents. Why is this? State **at least one** thing.
3 Raphael's father does not have a lot of time for him. Why is this? State **at least two** things.
4 Raphael talks about his father's behaviour. What does he say? State **at least three** things.
5 Now look at the text as a whole. Which of the following statements is correct? Tick **one** box.

| | |
|---|---|
| Vanessa and Raphael fall out with their parents regularly. | |
| Vanessa and Raphael get on well with their parents despite problems. | |
| Vanessa and Raphael get on extremely well with their parents. | |

# Learning

## Deutsche Sprache – schwere Sprache?

Susanne Zimmermann ist seit acht Jahren Lehrerin für Deutsch als Fremdsprache. Sie unterrichtet Jugendliche und Erwachsene aus anderen Nationen, die in Deutschland arbeiten möchten. Susannes Schüler sind alle älter als 18 Jahre, haben sich beim Jobcenter für diesen Deutschkurs angemeldet und wohnen bereits in Deutschland.

Jeder Integrationskurs dauert sechs Monate und Susannes Schüler müssen täglich fünf Stunden hart arbeiten, damit sie ihre Kenntnisse der deutschen Sprache sowie der deutschen Kultur, Geschichte und Politik erweitern. Am Ende haben alle Teilnehmer eine Prüfung und bekommen ein Zertifikat. Für einige Kursteilnehmer ist das eine schwere Aufgabe – besonders wenn sie den Kurs ohne Deutschkenntnisse beginnen.

„Ich habe schon 16 Nationen in einem Kurs gehabt – das ist manchmal nicht so einfach", sagt Susanne. „Aber es ist ein tolles Gefühl, wenn meine Schüler die Prüfung bestehen. Die Sprache ist das wichtigste Integrationsmittel und Voraussetzung für einen Arbeitsplatz in Deutschland."

Im Jahr 2012 sind fast eine Millionen Menschen aus anderen europäischen Ländern nach Deutschland gezogen. Jedes Jahr kommen mindestens eine halbe Millionen Einwanderer in die Bundesrepublik. Für Deutschlehrer wie Susanne Zimmermann gibt es auch in der Zukunft viel zu tun.

## Questions ?

1 Susanne Zimmermann is a teacher of German as a foreign language. Make notes in English under the following headings:
   - Susanne Zimmermann's students
   - Susanne Zimmermann's course
   - Susanne Zimmermann's opinion on her job
   - Susanne Zimmermann's job prospects in the future.

2 Now consider the passage as a whole. What does the text say about the importance of learning German? Tick the correct box.

| | |
|---|---|
| Learning German is not as important as learning about Germany. | |
| Learning German is necessary for work and life in Germany. | |
| Learning German is important for successful integration. | |

# Employability

## Traumberuf im Sommer?

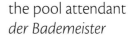

the pool attendant
*der Bademeister*

Christoph Graumann ist 25 Jahre alt und arbeitet seit neun Jahren im Freizeitbad seiner Heimatstadt Hannover. Dort hat er auch seine Ausbildung als Bademeister* gemacht, nachdem er die Realschule abgeschlossen hatte.

Wenn die Badegäste im Wasser planschen, passt Christoph auf, dass nichts passiert. Außerdem muss er jeden Morgen die Wassertemperatur kontrollieren und die Filter reinigen. In der Sommersaison muss Christoph auch andere Arbeiten erledigen – den Müll aufsammeln, die Toiletten sauber machen und sogar Eis verkaufen! Sehr oft sind seine Arbeitstage im Juli und August sehr lang.

„Meine Arbeit gefällt mir sehr – besonders dann, wenn die Sonne scheint und die meisten Besucher draußen im Freibad und nicht in der Schwimmhalle sind," sagt Christoph.

Obwohl er seinen Beruf liebt, hat er große Pläne für die Zukunft. Christoph würde sehr gern Sport studieren um Schwimmlehrer zu werden und in einem Verein junge Schwimmtalente zu trainieren. Da er sehr sportlich und fit ist, wünscht sich Christoph auch einen Start beim Iron-Man-Wettbewerb auf Hawaii. Bei diesem internationalen Wettbewerb muss er schwimmen, laufen und Fahrrad fahren. Dafür trainiert er täglich.

Musste er schon mal einen Schwimmer retten?

„Nein, hier im Freizeitbad nicht. Aber letzten Sommer habe ich an der Ostseeküste Ferien gemacht. Ein älterer Herr hatte seine Kraft überschätzt und hatte Probleme zum Strand zurück zu schwimmen. Ich habe das gesehen und konnte zum Glück helfen. Als Rettungsschwimmer ist man immer im Einsatz – auch in der Freizeit!"

## Questions ?

1. Christoph is 25 years old. Find **at least two** further personal details about him.
2. Christoph is a pool attendant. What exactly does his job involve? State **at least three** things.
3. What are Christoph's plans for the future? State **at least two** things.
4. Christoph talks about last summer. What does he say? Give **at least three** details.
5. Now consider the text as a whole. How does Christoph feel about his job? Tick the most appropriate box.

| | |
|---|---|
| Christoph loves his job but only when the sun shines. | |
| Christoph loves his job but wants to better himself. | |
| Christoph does not like his job and wants a career change. | |

# Culture

## Seifenopern im deutschen Fernsehen

Für deutsche Jugendliche sind Seifenopern genauso wichtig wie für ihre Altersgenossen in Großbritannien. Es gibt viele verschiedene Seifenopern im deutschen Fernsehen – für jeden ist etwas dabei. Vier deutsche Teenager stellen ihre Lieblingsseifenoper vor.

## Susanne (16 Jahre alt)

Also ich war ein Fan vom „Marienhof" und bin echt traurig, dass diese Seifenoper seit Juni 2011 nicht mehr gesendet wird. Die Geschichten im „Marienhof" waren immer sehr realistisch und es ging um die Probleme von ganz normalen Jugendlichen, die in einem Kölner Stadtteil lebten. Die familiäre Atmosphäre in der Seifenoper hat mir besonders gefallen.

## Mandy (18 Jahre alt)

Ich habe schon immer sehr gern „Verliebt in Berlin" gesehen. Die Hauptdarstellerin, Alexandra Neldel, finde ich einfach toll, weil sie die Rolle der Lisa super spielt. Sie zeigt, dass man sich von einer schüchternen und sogar tollpatschigen Person zu einer sehr attraktiven Person entwickeln kann. Ich denke, dass sich viele junge Mädchen mit dieser Rolle identifizieren.

## Thomas (19 Jahre alt)

Wenn meine Oma Seifenopern im Fernsehen angeschaut hat, fand ich das immer total langweilig. Aber jetzt sehe ich selber gern „Gute Zeiten, schlechte Zeiten", weil das eine Seifenoper ist, in der junge Menschen im Mittelpunkt stehen. Sie leben in Berlin – so wie ich – und gehen in die Schule, machen ein Studium oder ein Praktikum. GZSZ zeigt das Leben mit allen Höhen und Tiefen. Ich denke, die Geschichten sind sehr authentisch.

## Stephan (13 Jahre alt)

Ich sehe jeden Tag „Das Haus Anubis". Das ist die erste Seifenoper für Leute in meinem Alter. Ich finde die Geschichten spannend, denn es geht um Jugendliche, die in einem Internat wohnen. Das Haus hat ein Geheimnis, Leute verschwinden und es geht um einen Schatz. Echt gruselig!

## Questions ?

1 Who is it?
   a) This person likes horror and excitement.
   b) This person thinks that everybody can change.
   c) This person finds their granny's soap operas boring.
   d) This person's favourite soap opera is no longer on TV.
2 Why do Susanne, Mandy, Thomas and Stephan like their soap operas? State **at least two** things for each person.
3 Now consider the passage as a whole. According to the text, what role do soap operas play in the life of young people? Tick the most appropriate box.

| | |
|---|---|
| Soap operas help them to learn more about themselves and their teenage problems. | |
| Soap operas are good entertainment. | |
| Soap operas give them something to talk about. | |

# Listening Unit Assessment

# Society

## Monologue

Johanna is talking about her best friend Christine who used to be bullied in school.

## Questions

1 Johanna talks about her best friend.
   a) Why do they see each other a lot? State **at least two** things.
   b) Complete the following sentence: Christine is always _____ and _____ but she is never _____ .
2 Thomas does not like Christine. In what way does he show this? State **at least two** things.
3 The girls approach Frau Neumann, the class teacher. What does she do to help them? State **at least two** things.
4 Now consider the passage as a whole. What is the speaker's view on bullying? Tick the most appropriate box.

| | |
|---|---|
| Bullying is part of today's school culture. | |
| Bullying is not as serious as people think. | |
| Bullying needs to be discussed in today's schools. | |

# Learning

## Monologue

 *Bert is talking about his school problems.*

### Questions ?

1 Bert talks about his school. What does he say? State **at least three** things.
2 Maths is his favourite subject. Why is this? State **at least two** things.
3 His class teacher gives him advice on how to improve in History and Biology. What should Bert do? State **at least two** things.
4 Bert finds it difficult to make more time for school. Why is this? State **at least three** things.
5 Now consider the passage as a whole. What is Bert's view on school work? Tick the most appropriate box.

| | |
|---|---|
| Bert thinks that school work is not important. | |
| Bert thinks that spare time is as important as school. | |
| Bert thinks that school work is less important than spare time. | |

# Employability

## Dialogue

 *Sebastian and Anne are talking about work experience.*

### Questions ?

1 Anne talks about her work placement. What does she say? State **at least two** things.
2 Anne had some experience before she started her work placement. What kind of things did she do? State **at least one** thing.
3 What exactly does Anne do at her work placement? Give **at least three** details.
4 Anne finds her work stressful. Why is this? State **at least three** things.
5 What are Anne's plans for the future? Give **at least two** details.
6 Now consider the passage as a whole. What is Anne's view on her work experience? Tick the correct box.

| | |
|---|---|
| Anne thinks her work experience is a waste of time. | |
| Anne thinks her work experience is helpful. | |
| Anne thinks her work experience is fantastic. | |

# Culture

## Dialogue

 *Frank and Mandy live in a small town in Germany. They are talking about a class trip to Berlin next week.*

## Questions ?

1   Mandy is looking forward to the trip. Why is this? Give **at least two** details.
2   Frank asks about their accommodation. What does Mandy tell him? State **at least three** things.
3   Mandy talks about the trip programme. Complete the grid. Give **one** detail for each box.

| Day | Morning | Afternoon | Evening |
| --- | --- | --- | --- |
| **First Day** | | | |
| **Second Day** | | | |
| **Third Day** | | | |

4   Consider the passage as a whole. In what way has Frank prepared himself for the class trip to Berlin? Tick the most appropriate box.

| | |
| --- | --- |
| Frank is not interested in the trip at all. | |
| Frank is interested in the trip but has not read the programme. | |
| Frank is interested in the trip and has all the information. | |

# Listening transcripts

## Society

### Monologue

*Johanna is talking about her best friend Christine who used to be bullied in school.*

Seit vier Jahren habe ich eine super tolle beste Freundin, die Christine heißt und fünfzehn Jahre alt ist. Wir sehen uns oft, denn sie wohnt in meiner Straße. Seit einem Jahr gehen wir auch in eine Schule und in eine Klasse. Jeden Morgen treffen wir uns und fahren mit dem Rad zum Gymnasium.

Christine ist eine ganz tolle Freundin, denn sie ist immer freundlich und hilfsbereit – und niemals launisch. Außerdem ist sie die beste Schülerin in der Klasse und hat immer super Noten. Hausaufgaben sind für mich schon lange kein Problem mehr, weil wir sie zusammen machen.

Aber in unserer Klasse gibt es einen Jungen, der Thomas heißt. Er hänselt und ärgert Christine sehr oft, denn er sagt, dass sie klein und hässlich ist. Er hat das sogar auf ihre Facebook-Seite geschrieben! Das war ein totaler Schock für meine Freundin und wir haben überlegt, was man dagegen machen kann.

Christine und ich sind zu unserer Klassenlehrerin gegangen. Sie heißt Frau Neumann und wir finden sie alle ganz toll. Frau Neumann hat uns zugehört und Notizen gemacht. Dann hat sie mit Thomas gesprochen – sie hat ihm gesagt, dass er sich bei Christine entschuldigen muss. Eine Woche später haben wir in der Schule ein Projekt zum Thema 'Mobbing' gemacht. Das war sehr interessant aber auch schockierend. Ich bin der Meinung, dass Mobbing total doof ist und finde es absolut uncool. Niemand sollte mit einem Mobbing-Problem alleine sein. Es ist wichtig, dass man Freunde hat und auch eine erwachsene Person, der man vertrauen kann und die hilft.

## Learning

### Monologue

*Bert is talking about his school problems.*

Seit vier Jahren gehe ich in das Friedrich-Schiller-Gymnasium in Weimar. Ich bin in der zehnten Klasse und habe in diesem Jahr Prüfungen. Die zehnte Klasse ist echt hektisch und stressig, weil wir total viele Hausaufgaben haben und sehr viele Tests schreiben.

In Mathematik und Physik ist das kein Problem für mich, denn ich bin sehr gut in diesen Fächern. Mathe ist mein Lieblingsfach, weil ich gut logisch denken kann und mathematische Probleme schnell verstehe. Wenn ich mit der Schule fertig bin, würde ich sehr gern Mathe an der Universität studieren. Das Fach macht mir einfach Spaß.

Aber in Biologie und Geschichte muss ich sehr viel lernen und sehr viel machen. Manchmal geht mir das super auf die Nerven. Meine Lehrerin, Frau Hoffmann, sagt, ich soll meine Arbeit besser organisieren. Ich soll mehr Zeit mit den Hausaufgaben verbringen und vor einem Test mehr lernen. Aber das ist gar nicht so einfach!

Jeden Tag helfe ich meiner Mutter im Haus und mit meinem kleinen Bruder – er geht in den Kindergarten. Und in meiner Freizeit gehe ich gern mit meinen Freunden ins Kino oder in die Disko. Meine Freunde sind sehr wichtig für mich – ich möchte auch Zeit für sie haben und nicht nur über meinen Schulbüchern sitzen. Freizeit ist genauso wichtig wie Schule, denke ich.

# Employability
## Dialogue
*Sebastian and Anne are talking about work experience.*

| | |
|---|---|
| **Sebastian:** | Hallo Anne, wie geht's? |
| **Anne:** | Oh, Sebastian, hallo. Naja, es geht so. Ich mache gerade mein Arbeitspraktikum und das ist ganz schön stressig. |
| **Sebastian:** | Wo arbeitest du denn? |
| **Anne:** | Im Kindergarten. Dort bin ich jeden Tag sechs Stunden von neun Uhr bis fünfzehn Uhr. Morgen ist mein letzter Tag – zum Glück! |
| **Sebastian:** | Wieso denn? Gefällt dir die Arbeit mit Kindern nicht? |
| **Anne:** | Vor meinem Arbeitspraktikum habe ich gedacht, dass es mir Spaß macht, mit Kindern zu arbeiten. Ich habe ja auch schon öfter für meine Schwester den Babysitter gemacht – und auch bei den Nachbarn auf Kinder aufgepasst. Aber es ist schon etwas schwieriger, wenn man fünf bis zehn Kinder hat, mit denen man spielen soll. |
| **Sebastian:** | Was genau machst du denn eigentlich im Kindergarten? |
| **Anne:** | Naja, ich helfe bei Sportaktivitäten und mit dem Mittagessen. Außerdem singe ich mit den Kindern und wenn sie auf die Toilette müssen, gehe ich mit ihnen mit. Wir müssen darauf achten, dass jedes Kind die Toilette spült und sich die Hände wäscht und abtrocknet. Leider vergessen das die Kleinen relativ oft. |
| **Sebastian:** | Und warum findest du die Arbeit stressig? |

⇨

| Anne: | Es ist immer sehr laut im Kindergarten und man muss regelmäßig kontrollieren, ob alle Kinder in der Gruppe sind. Und jedes Kind hat seine eigenen Probleme und Besonderheiten, die man kennen muss. Ständig muss man aufräumen und irgendetwas sauber machen – Spielzeuge, Schuhe, Tische… die Arbeit ist nichts für mich. |
| --- | --- |
| Sebastian: | Was möchtest du denn später beruflich machen? |
| Anne: | Ich würde sehr gern mit Tieren arbeiten – entweder in einem Zoo oder in einem Tierheim. Vielleicht werde ich auch Hundetrainerin oder Tierärztin. So genau weiß ich das noch nicht. Das Arbeitspraktikum im Kindergarten hat mir geholfen zu erkennen, was ich später nicht machen möchte. |
| Sebastian: | Na siehst du – so schlecht war es dann doch nicht. |

# Culture

## Dialogue

*Frank and Mandy live in a small town in Germany. They are talking about a class trip to Berlin next week.*

| Frank: | Sag mal, Mandy, freust du dich schon auf die Klassenfahrt nach Berlin nächste Woche? |
| --- | --- |
| Mandy: | Ja, klar, total. Dann kommt man endlich mal raus aus dieser kleinen Stadt und sieht die große weite Welt! Berlin ist eine moderne Großstadt mit vielen Attraktionen und internationalem Flair. |
| Frank: | Ja, das stimmt. Weißt du eigentlich, wo wir wohnen werden? |
| Mandy: | Ja natürlich – im Brief an unsere Eltern steht, dass wir in einer kleinen Jugendherberge in der Stadtmitte wohnen werden. Wir haben Vierbettzimmer mit Dusche und das Frühstück ist inklusive. Die Jugendherberge ist in der Nähe vom Berliner Zoo. |
| Frank: | Ach so? Na dann ist das aber wirklich sehr zentral. Und was steht auf dem Programm? |
| Mandy: | Am ersten Tag machen wir morgens eine Stadtrundfahrt mit einem Bus. Wir besuchen am Nachmittag ein Museum und machen Fotos am Brandenburger Tor. Am Abend gehen wir in ein Restaurant am Alexanderplatz. |
| Frank: | Und was machen wir am zweiten Tag? |
| Mandy: | Das ist der sportliche Tag – wir gehen morgens ins Olympiastadion und nach dem Mittagessen besuchen wir die Berliner Eisbären beim Training – aber nicht im Zoo, sondern im Eisstadion beim Eishockey. |

⇨

⇒

**Frank:** Und am Abend?

**Mandy:** Mensch, Frank, du solltest wirklich einmal selber das Programm lesen – wir gehen in einen Club.

**Frank:** In einen Club? Mit den Lehrern? Das kann ja nur langweilig werden! Was machen wir am dritten Tag?

**Mandy:** Morgens haben wir Zeit zum Einkaufen im Eurocenter und danach gehen wir in den Zoo. Am Nachmittag besuchen wir das Holocaust Denkmal zwischen Brandenburger Tor und Potsdamer Platz. Und abends fahren wir zurück nach Hause.

**Frank:** Naja – da ist für jeden etwas dabei, denke ich. Vielen Dank für die Info, Mandy.

**Mandy:** Kein Problem.

### Hints & tips

*Before you tackle any of the following writing tasks for practice, remember these five guidelines for writing in German. Count them off on one hand to remind yourself:*

## 1 Plan your writing

*As in your English writing classes, you should carefully plan any piece of writing in German. It will help the readers to understand your views and thoughts much more easily and will help you to stay focused on the task.*

## 2 Expand on certain points and develop your thoughts

*Think about your German classes and which topics you have covered that could help you to produce a solid piece of writing in which you show what you are able to do.*

## 3 Avoid repetition

*Make sure you do not repeat words (nouns, verbs, pronouns, adjectives) but try to look for synonyms or alternative structures. You can also use inversion to avoid repetition at the beginning of a sentence.*

## 4 Express your opinion and provide a reason

*This can be done in a very simple way using **Ich finde** ... , **denn** ... However, for a National 5 award, try to show a sound knowledge of structures such as **Meiner Meinung nach** + verb ... , **weil** ...*

## 5 Check your writing

*Remember that all German nouns have a capital letter. Think about the correct verb ending (singular/plural) and tense form (present/perfect/future). You may use a dictionary for your writing.*

*Aim to write between 120 and 150 words. Do your best and try to give your writing some flair. Count your words before handing it in.*

# Society

## Planning your essay

Answer the questions in German and give some additional information, for example:

*Mein Freundeskreis ist relativ groß – ich habe etwa zehn gute Freunde. Sie wohnen in meiner Straße, in meiner Stadt, aber ich habe auch Facebook-Freunde in Australien und Irland.*

### Introduction

*Hast du einen großen oder kleinen Freundeskreis? Wo wohnen deine Freunde? Gehen sie in deine Schule?*

### Main part

*Wie heißt dein bester Freund/deine beste Freundin? Wie alt ist er/sie? Wie ist sein/ihr Charakter? Wo wohnt er/sie? Hat er/sie Geschwister? Was macht er/sie in der Freizeit?*

### Conclusion

*Warum ist er/sie dein bester Freund/deine beste Freundin? Ist Freundschaft wichtig für dich – oder ist Familie wichtiger?*

**Task**

Your German partner school is doing a project on friendship. They have asked you to write a paragraph in German about your best friend and what you think about friends and friendship.

## Sample essay suggestion

### Freunde und Freundschaft

Ich habe einen relativ großen Freundeskreis mit etwa zehn guten Freunden. Wir kennen uns seit Jahren, weil wir in einer Straße wohnen und in eine Schule gehen. Natürlich habe ich ein Facebook-Profil und etwa 200 Facebook-Freunde in Schottland, England, Frankreich und Deutschland.

Aber mein bester Freund heißt Connor und er geht in meine Klasse. Ich kenne ihn seit der Grundschule. Er wohnt in meiner Stadt und hat eine kleine Familie. Connor ist immer freundlich und nie launisch. Er ist hilfsbereit, wenn ich mit Hausaufgaben Probleme habe. Außerdem spielen wir zusammen in einem Fußballverein. Jede Woche haben wir zweimal Training. Connor interessiert sich auch sehr für Autos und Motorräder, weil er später Mechaniker werden möchte.

Ich denke, dass meine Freunde sehr wichtig sind, denn sie haben die gleichen Probleme und die gleichen Interessen wie ich.

**(140 words)**

# Learning

## Planning your essay

### Introduction

*Wie heißt deine Schule? Was für eine Schule ist das? Wie viele Schüler und Lehrer hat deine Schule?*

### Main part

*Wann beginnt und wann endet der Unterricht? Wie viele Stunden pro Tag hast du? Wie viele Pausen pro Tag hast du? Was ist dein Lieblingsfach? Welches Fach gefällt dir gar nicht? Wie sieht deine Schuluniform aus? Gibt es an deiner Schule Schultraditionen?*

### Conclusion

*Wie findest du deine Schule? Denkst du, dass Schule wichtig ist? Warum?*

**Task**

Your headteacher has asked you to produce a text about your school in German for the international section of your school website.

## Sample essay suggestion

### Meine Schule

Seit August 2012 besuche ich die Langholm Academy – das ist eine kleine Gesamtschule und Ganztagsschule im Süden von Schottland. Meine Schule hat etwa 200 Grundschüler und 300 Sekundarschüler.

Jeden Tag beginnt der Unterricht um neun Uhr und endet um halb vier. Wir haben sieben Stunden pro Tag, was ich total stressig finde. Es gibt morgens eine kleine Pause und mittags eine große Pause. Mein Lieblingsfach ist Kunst, weil ich sehr kreativ bin und es Spaß macht. Der Lehrer ist total toll, weil er immer Zeit für die Schüler hat. Sport gefällt mir gar nicht, denn ich bin unsportlich und finde Sport langweilig. Meine Schuluniform hat die Farben schwarz, weiß und kastanienbraun – echt altmodisch!

Meine Schule ist eine sehr gute Schule, denn die Atmosphäre ist familiär und locker, weil jeder jeden kennt. Ich gehe gern in die Langholm Academy.

**(140 words)**

# Employability

**Task**

Your German partner school has approached you and asked for a report in German about your work experience.

## Planning your essay

### Introduction

*Wann hast du dein Arbeitspraktikum gemacht? Wo hast du dein Arbeitspraktikum gemacht? Wie waren deine Arbeitszeiten?*

### Main Part

*Wie war es am ersten Tag? Was genau musstest du machen? Wer war dein Mentor? Bist du gut mit ihm/ihr ausgekommen? Wie waren die anderen Mitarbeiter?*

### Conclusion

*Wie hat dir dein Arbeitspraktikum gefallen? Möchtest du später in diesem Beruf arbeiten? Warum oder warum nicht?*

## Sample essay suggestion

### McDonalds – ich liebe es!

Im letzten Oktober habe ich ein Arbeitspraktikum in meiner Heimatstadt Glasgow gemacht. Ich habe eine Woche lang bei McDonalds im Stadtzentrum gearbeitet. Mein Arbeitstag hatte sechs Stunden – ich habe von 8 Uhr bis 14 Uhr gearbeitet und hatte eine halbe Stunde Pause.

Am ersten Tag war ich sehr nervös und aufgeregt, aber mein Mentor, Herr Buchanan, hat mir alles erklärt. Er war total geduldig und immer freundlich, obwohl das Restaurant oft sehr voll war.

Ich habe die Tische abgeräumt und abgewischt und Familien mit kleinen Kindern geholfen. Am besten haben mir die Geburtstagspartys gefallen, weil ich ein Kostüm getragen und Gesichter bemalt habe.

Ich bin sehr gut mit meinen Kollegen ausgekommen. Niemand war launisch oder unfreundlich.

Mein Arbeitspraktikum hat mir sehr gut gefallen, denn ich habe sehr viel über McDonalds gelernt. Das Restaurant ist ideal für Familien mit kleinen Kindern und für Leute, die schnell einen Kaffee und einen Imbiss möchten. Ich würde später sehr gern als Manager bei McDonalds arbeiten, weil man gut verdient und sehr gute Karrierechancen hat.

**(174 words)**

# Culture

## Planning your essay

### Introduction

*Siehst du viel oder wenig fern? Gehst du ins Kino oder siehst du lieber zu Hause fern? Hast du einen Fernseher in deinem Zimmer?*

**Task**

Your German partner school has asked you to write in German about your favourite film.

## Main part

*Wie heißt dein Lieblingsfilm? Ist das ein moderner oder älterer Film? Welches Thema hat der Film? Wer spielt die Hauptrolle? Wer spielt die Nebenrollen? Wo spielt der Film?*

## Conclusion

*Warum gefällt dir der Film? Was gefällt dir am besten am Film? Warum sollten andere Jugendliche diesen Film sehen?*

## Sample essay suggestion

### Film und Fernsehen

Fernsehen ist sehr wichtig für mich. Ich habe einen eigenen Fernseher in meinem Zimmer, sodass ich selbst entscheiden kann, was ich sehe. Ich sehe auch gern Filme im Kino, weil die Qualität besser ist und ich gern Popcorn esse!

Mein Lieblingsfilm heißt „Rose Red". Das ist ein Horrorfilm nach einem Buch von Stephen King. Der Film stammt aus dem Jahr 1998 und die Handlung spielt in Seattle. Eine Gruppe von sieben Personen verbringt ein Wochenende in einem Geisterhaus, wo Menschen verschwinden. Die Hauptrolle spielt Nancy Travis – sie ist eine brilliante aber sehr ehrgeizige Professorin.

Der Film gefällt mir, weil er spannend und überraschend ist. Es geht im Film um Liebe und Ehrgeiz, um Freundschaft und Vertrauen, um Gut und Böse. Rose Red ist ein Horrorfilm der anderen Art – interessant und philosophisch.

**(134 words)**

# Talking Unit Assessment

## Hints & tips

*Before you start tackling the speaking tasks for practice, remember that you achieve best with a strategy:*

- *Answer each question but either try to add another detail or piece of information and/or express an opinion.*
- *Go beyond a minimal response and make sure that you speak German all the time and do not slip into English.*
- *Do not panic if you don't understand a question. Your teacher knows you well and will support you.*

### Example

**Question:** *Wo genau wohnst du?*

**Good answer:** *Ich wohne in Edinburgh. Das ist die Hauptstadt von Schottland.*

**Better answer:** *Ich wohne in der Hauptstadt Edinburgh. Die Stadt liegt an der Küste im Osten von Schottland. Meine Familie wohnt in einem Haus am Stadtrand.*

# Society

## Sample questions

Here are some questions you should be able to answer:

- *Hast du viel oder wenig Freizeit?*
- *Was machst du in deiner Freizeit?*
- *Was machst du normalerweise am Wochenende?*
- *Wofür interessierst du dich besonders?*
- *Welche Rolle spielen moderne Medien in deiner Freizeit?*
- *Hast du ein Lieblingshobby?*
- *Denkst du, dass Freizeit wichtig ist?*

## Suggested sample answers

- Im Moment habe ich nicht so viel Freizeit, weil ich sehr viel für die Schule lernen muss und mehr Zeit mit Hausaufgaben verbringe. Ich werde im Mai meine Prüfungen machen.
- Wenn ich Freizeit habe, sehe ich sehr gern fern. Ich habe meinen eigenen Fernseher in meinem Zimmer, sodass ich meine Sendungen wählen kann. Am liebsten sehe ich Seifenopern und Musiksendungen.
- Am Wochenende treffe ich meine Freunde und wir fahren in die Stadtmitte, wo wir ins Kino oder in die Pizzeria gehen. Außerdem spiele ich manchmal Tennis oder ich gehe ins Hallenbad.

⇨

### Task

You are taking part in a German event about "Jugend und Freizeit" at the Goethe Institut Glasgow. The other participants ask you questions in German about your hobbies and spare-time activities

⇨

- Ich interessiere mich besonders für Sport, weil ich sehr sportlich bin und fit bleiben möchte. Meine Lieblingssportart ist Schwimmen, denn es entspannt und ist gesund. Aber ich spiele auch sehr gern Fußball.
- Moderne Medien spielen eine sehr große Rolle für mich. Ich habe ein Handy, einen Laptop und verschiedene Spielkonsolen. Meistens chatte ich mit Freunden online oder wir spielen Computerspiele. Das finde ich total cool.
- Nein, ich würde nicht sagen, dass ich ein Lieblingshobby habe. Aber ich höre sehr gern Musik.
- Ich denke, dass Freizeit sehr wichtig ist. Man muss einen Ausgleich zur Schule haben und man sollte auch Zeit für die eigenen Interessen haben.

# Learning

## Sample questions

Here are some questions you should be able to answer:

- *Was für eine Schule besuchst du?*
- *In welche Klasse gehst du?*
- *Wann beginnt und wann endet der Schultag?*
- *Welche Fächer lernst du in der Schule?*
- *Hast du ein Lieblingsfach?*
- *Wie findest du Schuluniform?*
- *Möchtest du studieren oder eine Lehre machen?*

**Task**

You are at your German partner school. The teacher asks you about your school and school life in Scotland.

## Suggested sample answers

- Seit August 2012 besuche ich die High School in Dumfries. Das ist eine Gesamtschule mit etwa 900 Schülern.
- Im Moment lerne ich in der S4 – das ist die zehnte Klasse in Deutschland. Nächstes Jahr mache ich meine mittlere Reife.
- Mein Schultag beginnt um neun Uhr und endet um halb vier. Ich finde das zu lang – besonders am Freitag, wenn man Wochenende hat und wegfahren möchte.
- Ich lerne natürlich die Pflichtfächer Englisch, Mathematik, Sport, Religion und Sozialkunde. Außerdem habe ich meine Wahlfächer Physik, Deutsch, Technisches Zeichnen, Politik und Geschichte.
- Mein Lieblingsfach ist Deutsch, weil es relativ einfach zu verstehen ist. Aber ich finde Physik auch toll, denn wir machen viele Experimente.
- Schuluniform ist eine Tradition in Schottland. Ich finde sie praktisch, denn man muss nicht lange überlegen, was man anzieht.
- Später möchte ich gern eine Lehre als Elektriker machen. Ich würde gern Lehrling in einer Firma sein und zur Berufsschule gehen.

# Employability

## Sample questions

- *Erzählen Sie etwas über sich.*
- *Was sind Ihre Stärken?*
- *Wo im Freizeitpark würden Sie gern arbeiten?*
- *Warum möchten Sie in Deutschland arbeiten?*
- *Welche Sprachen sprechen Sie?*
- *Haben Sie andere Qualifikationen?*
- *Wie viele Wochen können Sie für uns arbeiten?*

**Task**

You have applied for a summer job in a theme park in Germany and have been invited to a telephone interview.

## Suggested sample answers

- Ich heiße Brian Kennedy und bin 17 Jahre alt. Seit meiner Geburt wohne ich in Inverness. Im Moment besuche ich eine Gesamtschule. In meiner Freizeit mache ich sehr viel Sport, weil ich sehr fit bin. Am liebsten mache ich Wassersport, ich fahre sehr gern Kanu und ich schwimme sehr gern.

- Ich denke, dass ich freundlich und höflich bin. Meine Freunde sagen, dass ich gerne helfe und zuverlässig bin. Und meine Lehrer sind der Meinung, dass ich sehr gut arbeiten kann, weil ich fleißig bin. Ich arbeite sehr gern im Team, aber ich kann Probleme auch alleine lösen.

- Ich würde sehr gern etwas Sportliches machen oder etwas verkaufen – Tickets zum Beispiel. Ich kann aber auch in einem Café arbeiten oder in einem Restaurant helfen.

- Ich möchte gern in Deutschland arbeiten, weil ich das Land und die Leute kennen lernen will. Außerdem würde ich gern mein Deutsch verbessern.

- Englisch ist meine Muttersprache. Ich lerne seit fünf Jahren Deutsch und seit sieben Jahren Französisch. Außerdem verstehe ich etwas Holländisch und Spanisch.

- Vor einem Jahr habe ich eine Segelqualifikation gemacht und im Moment mache ich meine Fahrerlaubnis. Außerdem habe ich ein Erste-Hilfe-Zertifikat.

- Ich kann sechs bis acht Wochen in Ihrem Freizeitpark arbeiten – dann muss ich wieder zurück nach Schottland, weil mein Studium beginnt.

# Culture

## Sample questions

Here are some questions you should be able to answer:
- *Siehst du viel oder wenig fern?*
- *Hast du einen eigenen Fernseher in deinem Zimmer?*
- *Gehst du gern ins Kino oder siehst du lieber eine DVD?*
- *Wann warst du das letzte Mal im Kino?*
- *Was siehst du gern im Fernsehen?*
- *Was siehst du gar nicht gern im Fernsehen?*
- *Hast du einen Lieblingsfilm?*

**Task**

Your German partner school is doing a survey on TV habits. They have asked you to take part.

# Suggested sample answers

- Ich sehe sehr viel fern – jeden Tag so etwa zwei bis drei Stunden.
- Ja, ich habe einen eigenen Fernseher in meinem Zimmer. Er hat auch ein DVD-Teil, sodass ich meine Lieblingsfilme sehen kann.
- Naja, ich gehe schon gern ins Kino, aber es ist manchmal ein bisschen teuer. Am liebsten sehe ich mit meinen Freunden DVDs.
- Das letzte Mal war ich vor drei Monaten im Kino. Wir sind mit der Klasse gegangen und haben einen Film auf Deutsch gesehen – mit englischen Untertiteln. Es hat mir gut gefallen.
- Ich sehe sehr gern Dokumentarfilme, weil man etwas lernen kann und die weite Welt sieht.
- Also ich finde Talentshows total furchtbar, weil die meisten Leute kein Talent haben und nur peinlich sind.
- Ja, mein Lieblingsfilm ist „Appollo 13" mit Tom Hanks in der Hauptrolle. Ich finde alle Tom Hanks Filme echt super, denn sie haben Qualität.

# What you should know about the National 5 German Course Assessment

Compared to the unit assessments which are marked as pass/fail, the course assessment will be graded. The grade depends on the number of marks you are able to achieve across all four skills:

- **Reading:** out of 30 marks
- **Writing:** out of 20 marks
- **Listening:** out of 20 marks
- **Talking:** out of 30 marks

If you achieve 70 marks or more, you will be likely to get an 'A' in your N5 German course assessment. You need at least 50 marks to get a 'C' which equals a 'Pass'.

So – how do we get there?

## Können wir das schaffen?

*Ja, wir schaffen das!*

# Reading Course Assessment 📖

This assessment counts for 30 marks. You will read three German texts of between 150 and 200 words each. Questions on the text are set in English, and you must respond in English. These questions will ask for specific details about the text but there will also be an 'overall purpose' question which is the literacy element and shows your holistic (full) understanding of the text. You may use a dictionary in this paper.

## Hints & tips ⭐

### Before you read the German texts

✓ Read the title/headline and ask yourself what you already know about the topic.

✓ Look at any pictures as they support the content of a text.

✓ Check if the text comes with a glossary to save yourself time looking up words in the dictionary.

### While you are reading the German texts

✓ Focus on your reading – be an active reader!

✓ Try to figure out the main idea(s) of the text(s).

✓ Access the meaning of a word by:

checking the context/sentence of the word

checking if the word is similar to English (German and English have many cognates or near cognates – see Chapter 1)

checking whether or not the text comes with a glossary

using a dictionary.

### After you have read the text and before you start answering the questions

✓ Read the comprehension questions carefully.

✓ If necessary, underline the question word to highlight exactly what kind of answer is required.

✓ Check the tense form of the English question to make sure you use the same tense form in your answer.

✓ Make sure that your answer has sufficient detail – compare it with the marks you can get for each answer.

Most importantly – make sure your English answers make sense and your English expression is of a good standard. Allow yourself time to go over your answers once you have finished your work.

Here are some example course assessments for you to practise on.

# Society

## Sport ist mehr als gesund

Sport und Fitness spielen eine große Rolle für Teenager in Deutschland. Mehr als 60% der 12-jährigen und etwa 40% der 18-jährigen Jugendlichen in Deutschland sind Mitglied in einem Sportverein. Sie treffen sich regelmäßig zum Training und verbringen sehr viel Freizeit in ihren Klubs.

In Sportvereinen können Kinder und Jugendliche soziale Erfahrungen mit Gleichaltrigen machen und Spaß an Bewegung haben. Besonders wichtig sind Gruppenaktivitäten und Wettkämpfe, bei denen man Ehrlichkeit, Fairness, die Einhaltung von Regeln, Solidarität und Partnerschaft lernt.

Außerdem organisieren Sportklubs sehr oft Feste – zu Weihnachten zum Beispiel oder zu Silvester. Und im Sommer gibt es regelmäßig Feriencamps, Tagesfahrten und extra Training für Sporttalente – also viele Gelegenheiten neue Freunde zu finden.

Und wer wirklich großes Interesse an einer Sportkarriere hat, kann Mannschaftssprecher werden oder eine Ausbildung zum Übungsleiter machen.

Wenn man Mitglied in einem Sportverein ist, tut man nicht nur etwas für die Gesundheit. Man lernt tolerant zu sein, Konflikte zu lösen, andere Jugendliche und Erwachsene zu verstehen und Verantwortung zu übernehmen. Sport ist nicht nur gesund, sondern bietet Gelegenheit zum sozialen Lernen.

## Questions

1 Sport is important for German teenagers. What evidence is there for this? Give **any one** detail. **(1)**
2 Group activities are very important in a club. Why is this? Give **any three** details. **(3)**
3 What other events do sport clubs usually organise? State **any two** things. **(2)**
4 According to the text, members of sport clubs learn personal skills. What exactly do they learn? State **any three** things. **(3)**
5 Now consider the passage as a whole. What is the author's view on sport clubs? Tick the most appropriate box. **(1)**

| | |
|---|---|
| Sport clubs help teenagers to develop sports skills. | |
| Sport clubs are not necessary for teenagers to enjoy exercise. | |
| Sport clubs offer fitness and opportunities for social learning. | |

# Learning

## Hausaufgaben – nein, danke?

Sarah besucht die Friedrich-Schiller-Gesamtschule in Weimar und geht in die neunte Klasse. Im Unterricht haben die Schüler das Thema „Hausaufgaben" diskutiert. Sarah sagt dazu ihre Meinung:

„Die meisten Schüler in meiner Klasse machen ihre Hausaufgaben nur, weil sie sonst eine schlechte Note bekommen, nach dem Unterricht in der Schule bleiben müssen oder die Eltern informiert werden – und dann gibt es Krach zu Hause!

In vielen Fächern sind die Hausaufgaben sinnlos, weil die Lehrer die Aufgaben nicht richtig kontrollieren und oft schon zufrieden sind, dass die Hausaufgaben überhaupt gemacht wurden. Man kann also nicht feststellen, ob man etwas richtig oder falsch beantwortet hat. Und nicht selten vergessen die Lehrer, dass sie Hausaufgaben erteilt haben.

Es gibt aber auch Lehrer, die total schwierige Hausaufgaben aufgeben, sodass man Hilfe braucht. Das ist ein Nachteil für Familien, die ihren Kindern keine Privatlehrer bezahlen können, weil das ein finanzielles Problem ist. Oder die Eltern arbeiten beide Vollzeit und kommen abends sehr spät nach Hause und haben dann keine Zeit bei den Hausaufgaben zu helfen. Diese Kinder sind natürlich im Nachteil.

Meiner Meinung nach sollten Hausaufgaben nicht so oft erteilt werden. Die Lehrer können nicht jede Woche die Hausaufgaben von 150 Schülern mit nach Hause nehmen und korrigieren. Dann hätten sie keine Zeit für die Vorbereitung des Unterrichts und müssten rund um die Uhr arbeiten. Aber wenn Hausaufgaben erteilt werden, dann sollten sie logisch in den Unterricht integriert sein."

## Questions ?

1 According to Sarah, why do most students do homework? Give **any two** details. **(2)**
2 Sarah says that in many subjects homework is meaningless. Why is this? State **any three** things. **(3)**
3 What problems are there when homework is too difficult? State **any two** things. **(2)**
4 In what way does homework impact on teachers? Give **any two** details. **(2)**
5 Now consider the passage as a whole. What is Sarah's view on homework? Tick the most appropriate box. **(1)**

| | |
|---|---|
| Sarah is against homework. | |
| Sarah is in favour of homework on a regular basis. | |
| Sarah wants homework to be meaningful and manageable. | |

# Employability

## Traumberuf Tierarzt?

Das Thema „Beruf" ist für Kinder sehr wichtig. Sie lieben es über die Zukunft zu sprechen und sehen sich gern als Erwachsene in spannenden Jobs. Sehr oft kommen ihre Ideen aus Literatur, Film oder Fernsehen.

Sehr viele Jungen und Mädchen in Deutschland möchten gern Tierarzt oder Tierärztin werden, weil sie davon träumen Tiere gesund zu machen, Tieren bei Schmerzen zu helfen oder den ganzen Tag mit süßen Haustieren zu kuscheln. Doch die Realität sieht ganz anders aus.

Ein Tierarzt muss oft mit nervösen oder aggressiven Tieren umgehen. Die meisten Tierärzte arbeiten in der Landwirtschaft – in einem Kuhstall, Schweinestall oder auf einer Hühnerfarm. Und manchmal muss man ein Tier einschläfern, weil es zu krank ist oder zu starke Schmerzen hat. Dafür braucht man starke Nerven und das Verständnis, dass man dem Tier hilft.

Wenn man kein Blut sehen kann, Angst vor Tieren hat oder keinen Stress im Job haben möchte, sollte man kein Tierarzt werden. Die Ausbildung dauert auch ziemlich lange – man muss fünf Jahre lang Tiermedizin studieren, bevor man eine Stelle in einer Tierpraxis bekommt. Außerdem muss man sehr oft am Wochenende und im Schichtdienst arbeiten.

Für alle, die solche Probleme nicht scheuen, kann der Beruf sehr schön sein.

## Questions ?

1 The topic 'job' is important for children. Why is this? Give **any one** detail. **(1)**
2 Many boys and girls in Germany want to be a vet. What do they dream about? State **any two** things. **(2)**
3 In what way is the reality for vets different? State **any three** things. **(3)**
4 What kind of people should not become a vet? Give **any three** details. **(3)**
5 Now consider the passage as a whole. What is the author's view on a vet's job? Tick the most appropriate box. **(1)**

| | |
|---|---|
| Being a vet is a demanding job. | |
| Being a vet is not a dream job. | |
| Being a vet can be a dream job for the right person. | |

# Culture

## Ferien mit Teenagern

Viele Jugendliche in Deutschland träumen von Ferien mit ihren Freunden. Sie wollen nicht mehr mit den Eltern in Urlaub fahren, weil sie andere Interessen haben und unabhängig sein wollen. Außerdem möchten sie morgens lange schlafen und lieber im Zelt als in einem Hotel wohnen.

Was sollten Eltern tun, die mit Kindern im Teenageralter in den Urlaub fahren wollen?

Bevor es überhaupt los geht, sollten sie die Reise gemeinsam mit ihren Kindern planen. Es ist wichtig, dass sie die Wünsche der Jugendlichen verstehen und respektieren. Junge Leute sind nicht gern allein – also sollten die Eltern vielleicht einen Freund oder eine Freundin einladen.

Wenn es um die Unterkunft geht, ist ein Ferienhaus in der Nähe einer Stadt ideal für Ferien mit der Familie. Das Haus sollte groß sein und einen Garten haben. Die Jugendlichen brauchen ein eigenes Zimmer, welches sie zur „elternfreien Zone" erklären können. Wenn das Haus dann auch noch einen Fernseher und einen Internetanschluss hat, ist der Urlaub perfekt.

Man muss nicht unbedingt auf die Partyinsel Mallorca fahren, damit Jugendliche tolle Ferien verbringen können. Ein Sommerurlaub an der Ostsee mit Sonne, Sand und Meer sowie Strandpartys und Wassersport ist ein Hit bei deutschen Jugendlichen.

Ferien mit der ganzen Familie sind kein Problem, wenn alle Familienmitglieder kompromissbereit sind und Verständnis für einander haben.

## Questions

1   Many young Germans dream about holidays with their friends. Why is this? State **any two** things. **(2)**

2   What should parents do if they want to go on holiday with their teenage kids? Give **any two** details. **(2)**

3   According to the passage, what kind of accommodation is ideal for families? Give **any three** details. **(3)**

4   German teenagers like holidays at the Baltic Sea. Why is this? Give **any two** details. **(2)**

5   Consider the passage as a whole. What is the author's view on family holidays with teenagers? Tick the most appropriate box. **(1)**

| | |
|---|---|
| Teenagers should not go on holiday with their parents anymore. | |
| Teenagers should follow their parents' holiday plans. | |
| Teenagers and their views should be considered by parents before and during the holiday. | |

# Chapter 10

# Listening Course Assessment

This assessment counts for 20 marks. You will listen to one monologue (approximately one and a half minutes long) and one short dialogue (approximately two to two and a half minutes long) in German. You will be asked questions in English and must respond in English.

The monologue is worth 8 marks and it is necessary for you to understand the overall purpose of the spoken text (see Chapter 9, Reading Course Assessment and Page 5). The dialogue is worth 12 marks and it has a topical link to the monologue.

You may **not** use a dictionary in this paper.

## Hints & tips ⭐

*Learn your vocabulary regularly and revise systematically before the exam. Only those who recognise words will be able to understand the meaning of a spoken sentence.*

### Before your listening exam

✓ *Revise vocabulary, especially verbs in their different tense forms, quantifiers* **(viel, wenig, die meisten)***, numbers and dates. Read vocabulary out loud so that you can audibly recognise what you see in front of you.*

✓ *Read the title/introduction to the listening item and ask yourself what experience you have of this topic and what you know about it.*

✓ *Remember the close relationship between the English and the German language where many words sound very similar and use this to your benefit in listening. However, beware:* **Schinken** *is not 'chicken'!*

✓ *Read the English questions very carefully — you have one minute to study them — and underline the question words or any others which you feel might be of importance.*

✓ *Remember that the questions are in chronological sequence — the answer to question (c) must be between the answers to (b) and (d) in the recording.*

### While you are sitting your listening exam

✓ *Remember that both items (monologue and dialogue) will be played three times so it is not necessary to answer any questions the first time.*

✓ *Write your answers neatly and clearly on your question paper. If you correct your answer, make sure the examiner will be able to recognise your final answer.*

✓ *If you don't understand a word which you believe to be an element of an answer — don't panic! Trust your instinct and your natural connection to German as a speaker of English and see if you can guess the meaning.*

✓ *Be guided by the number of marks allocated to each question. They will tell you how much information is expected in your answer.* ⇨

⇨

## After your listening exam

✓ *Go over your answers. Make sure that what you have written in English is as clear as possible.*

✓ *Make sure you have crossed out any draft answers, leaving only the final answer for the examiner to see.*

# Society

## Monologue

 *Caroline, a German teenager, talks about her family.*

### Questions ?

1 Caroline's family is very large. What evidence is there in the passage? State **any one** thing.
2 It was difficult for the family to find accommodation. Why was that? State **any two** things.
3 Caroline's parents decided to buy a house. What does she tell us about it? State **any three** things.
4 How do the children get to school now? State **any one** thing.
5 Now consider the passage as a whole. What is Caroline's view on life in a large family? Tick the most appropriate box.

| | |
|---|---|
| Caroline finds life in a large family problematic. | |
| Caroline loves life in a large family despite some problems. | |
| Caroline prefers a small family to a large family. | |

# Society

## Dialogue

 *A local radio station in Rostock is interviewing Caroline's brother Jörg about the daily routine in a family of eight.*

### Questions ?

1 Jörg says he gets on very well with his siblings. Why is this? Give **any two** details.
2 Jörg talks about helping at home.
   a) How does the family organise their chores? Give **any one** detail.
   b) What are Jörg's duties? State **any two** things.
3 Life in a big family is different. What examples does Jörg give for this? State **any two** things.
4 According to Jörg, going camping is ideal for a big family. Why is this? Give **any three** details.
5 Jörg talks about his plans for the future. What does he say? State **any one** thing.

# Learning

## Monologue

🔊 *Andreas, a German teenager, is talking about his school career.*

### Questions ❓

1   Andreas has always liked school. Why is this? Give **any two** details.
2   He found grammar school difficult at first. In what way was it different from primary school? State **any three** things.
3   Andreas talks about his career in further education. What does he say? State **any two** things.
4   Now consider the passage as a whole. What is Andreas' opinion about education? Tick the most appropriate box.

| | |
|---|---|
| Andreas thinks that education helps him to achieve his life dreams. | |
| Andreas thinks that education is not as important as family support. | |
| Andreas thinks that education does not change a person's lifestyle. | |

# Learning

## Dialogue

🔊 *Andreas and his sister Mandy are talking about school and spare time.*

### Questions ❓

1   Mandy has not done her homework yet. Why is this? State **any two** things.
2   Mandy talks about the amount of homework she gets. What does she say? Give **any two** details.
3   Mandy cannot meet her best friend Nancy very often. Why is this? State **any two** things.
4   Mandy talks about her hobbies.
    **a)** Why does she like playing the guitar? State **any two** things.
    **b)** What does she like about the sports club? State **any one** thing.
5   Mandy is able to cope with homework and hobbies. What does she do to achieve this? Give **any three** details.

# Employability

## Monologue

🔊 *Markus talks about his experience of a job interview for a summer job.*

### Questions ?

1  According to Markus, it is not easy to find a part-time job in the summer. Why is this? Give **any two** details.
2  Markus had help to prepare for the job interview.
   **a)** In what way did his German teacher help him? State **any one** thing.
   **b)** In what way did his parents help him? State **any one** thing.
3  Markus talks about the day of the job interview. What does he say? Give **any three** details.
4  Now consider the passage as a whole. How does Markus feel about his achievement? Tick the most appropriate box.

| | |
|---|---|
| Markus feels he has deserved this job. | |
| Markus feels that he has been very lucky to get this job. | |
| Markus feels nervous about his first part-time job. | |

# Employability

## Dialogue

🔊 *Markus and Anita are talking about Anita's work experience.*

### Questions ?

1  Anita says that working in a restaurant is not for her. Why is this? State **any two** things.
2  What exactly did Anita do in the restaurant? Give **any three** details.
3  How did she get on with staff? State **any two** things.
4  Anita talks about her contact with guests. What does she say? State **any two** things.
5  What are Anita's plans for the future? Give **any one** detail.
6  According to Anita, why is work experience a good idea? State **any two** things.

# Culture

## Monologue

 *Christine talks about her holiday plans.*

**Questions**

1. Christine is looking forward to her holiday with friends. Why is this? State **any one** thing.
2. Christine and her friends will spend three weeks at the Baltic Sea coast. What does she tell us about their accommodation? Give **any three** details.
3. Christine is particularly interested in the city of Rostock. Why is this? Give **any two** details.
4. According to Christine, why were her holidays with her parents problematic? State **any one** thing.
5. Now consider the passage as a whole. What is Christine's view on holidays without parents? Tick the most appropriate box.

| | |
|---|---|
| Christine thinks that holidays without parents are difficult to organise. | |
| Christine thinks that holidays without parents are a chance to get to know young people. | |
| Christine thinks that holidays without parents are a good preparation for life. | |

# Culture

## Dialogue

 *Stefan and Christine talk about a long weekend in Berlin.*

**Questions**

1. Stefan and his friends will spend a long weekend in Berlin. What does he say about the travel arrangements? Give **any two** details.
2. What exactly did Stefan do to organise the trip? State **two** things.
3. Stefan talks about the programme for the weekend.
   a) What does he say about Saturday? State **any two** things.
   b) What does he say about Sunday? State **any one** thing.
4. Stefan talks about his parents and their view on the Berlin trip. What does he say? State **any three** things.
5. What is Stefan's dream destination? State **any one** place.
6. In what way did Stefan and his friends raise money for their Berlin weekend? Give **any one** detail.

# Listening transcripts

# Society

## Monologue

*Caroline, a German teenager, talks about her family.*

Ich heiße Caroline und ich bin 15 Jahre alt. Meine Familie ist sehr groß: Ich habe einen Bruder, einen Stiefbruder, zwei Schwestern und eine Stiefschwester – wir sind also zusammen mit meiner Mutter und meinem Stiefvati acht Personen. Das kann manchmal ganz schön nervig sein.

Als meine Mutter meinen Stiefvati geheiratet hat, mussten wir eine größere Wohnung finden. Das war gar nicht so einfach, denn viele Leute denken, dass sechs Kinder zu viel Krach machen und dass große Familien keine Ordnung halten können. Außerdem haben wir noch zwei Hunde und zwei Autos, die einen Parkplatz brauchen.

Meine Eltern haben dann beschlossen, ein Haus auf dem Land zu kaufen. Wir wohnen jetzt alle in einem Einfamilienhaus in der Nähe von Rostock. Das ist im Nordosten von Deutschland. Das Haus ist super groß, jedes Kind hat ein eigenes Zimmer und wir haben einen großen Garten, wo wir mit den Hunden spielen können. Ein Bus oder mein Stiefvati bringt uns jeden Morgen in die Schule und am Wochenende in die Disko und zum Einkaufen.

Das Leben in einer Großfamilie ist nie langweilig; es ist immer jemand da, mit dem man reden kann, wenn man ein Problem hat. Ich kann mir nicht vorstellen, ohne meine Familie zu sein und wenn ich älter bin, möchte ich auch gern eine große Familie haben.

# Society

## Dialogue

*A local radio station in Rostock is interviewing Caroline's brother Jörg about the daily routine in a family of eight.*

[Caroline] Hallo Jörg, danke, dass du ins Studio gekommen bist. Du hast fünf Geschwister – kommst du gut mit ihnen aus?

[Jörg] Oh ja, wir verstehen uns sehr gut – aber manchmal gibt es kleine Probleme, wenn wir zum Bespiel Freunde nach Hause bringen wollen oder eine Party machen möchten. Zum Glück haben wir vier Fernseher und jeder hat ein kleines Netbook oder einen Laptop, sodass wir uns nicht streiten, wer wann im Internet surfen darf.

[Caroline] Hilfst du deiner Familie im Haushalt?

[Jörg] Ja, wir alle müssen helfen. Meine Mutter ist die Managerin der Familie. Sie stellt jedes Wochenende einen Plan für die nächste Woche auf. Außerdem hat sie einen Kalender für die ganze Familie, damit wir keine Termine vergessen. Ich muss meistens Staub saugen, die Hunde füttern und mit ihnen Gassi gehen.

[Caroline] Gibt es Unterschiede im Alltag zwischen großen und kleinen Familien?

[Jörg] Oh ja, das Leben in einer großen Familie ist schon anders. Wenn wir im Supermarkt einkaufen gehen, brauchen wir normalerweise zwei Einkaufswagen. Die Leute gucken dann immer total komisch – aber ein Einkaufswagen ist einfach nicht groß genug. Außerdem haben wir drei Waschmaschinen und einen Kleinbus als Familienauto.

[Caroline] Und wie ist das, wenn ihr in die Ferien fahrt?

[Jörg] Naja, die Ferien müssen wir immer gut planen und organisieren. Am besten sind Ferien auf einem Campingplatz, weil wir dann alle zusammen wohnen können und auch die Hunde kommen mit. Außerdem gibt es viel Platz, wir können selber kochen und müssen nicht so viel Geld ausgeben.

[Caroline] Möchtest du später auch eine große Familie haben?

[Jörg] Also ehrlich gesagt, ich möchte erst einmal einen guten Job finden und die Welt kennen lernen. Da ich noch nie im Ausland gewesen bin, würde ich sehr gern einmal nach Afrika oder Asien reisen. Andere Länder und Kulturen faszinieren mich. Sicher möchte ich einmal eine Partnerin und eventuell ein oder zwei Kinder – aber das hat noch Zeit.

[Caroline] Vielen Dank, Jörg, dass du ins Studio gekommen bist.

[Jörg] Bitte, gern geschehen.

# Learning

## Monologue

*Andreas, a German teenager, is talking about his school career.*

Ich bin schon immer sehr gern in die Schule gegangen. Das Lernen macht mir Spaß, weil meine Lehrer geduldig und nie launisch sind sowie viel Verständnis für meine Interessen haben.

Mit sechs Jahren bin ich in die Grundschule gekommen. Dort war ich vier Jahre, bevor ich dann auf die Sekundarschule gewechselt bin. Ich war ein sehr guter Schüler, sodass ich zum Gymnasium gehen konnte. Das war am Anfang sehr schwierig, denn in der Grundschule hatten wir nicht so viele Hausaufgaben und haben meistens gesungen und gespielt. Außerdem hatten wir am Gymnasium verschiedene Lehrer und mussten jede Stunde das Klassenzimmer wechseln. Trotzdem habe ich nicht aufgegeben und meine Eltern haben mich immer unterstützt, wenn es Probleme gab.

In diesem Jahr werde ich mein Abitur machen. Danach würde ich sehr gern an einer Universität studieren, um Ingenieur zu werden. In meiner Familie bin ich dann der Erste, der einen Universitätsabschluss haben wird.

Ich interessiere mich sehr für Flugzeuge und Helicopter. Da ich am Gymnasium zwei Fremdsprachen gelernt habe, möchte ich auf jeden Fall ein Jahr im Ausland studieren. Ich denke, dass Schule wichtig für das Leben ist – man sollte jeden Tag gut nutzen, damit man später seine Träume realisieren kann.

# Learning

## Dialogue

*Andreas and his sister Mandy are talking about school and spare time.*

**[Andreas]** Sag mal, Mandy, hast du deine Hausaufgaben schon gemacht?

**[Mandy]** Nee… noch nicht. Erstmal bin ich mit dem Hund Gassi gegangen, danach habe ich ein Paket von der Post geholt und dann hat Mutti auf dem Handy angerufen und mich in den Supermarkt geschickt, um Milch zu kaufen.

**[Andreas]** Hast du denn viele Hausaufgaben auf?

**[Mandy]** Naja, geht so. Mathe und Deutsch ist immer richtig viel. Ich denke mal, weil das Hauptfächer sind. Aber wir haben auch jede Woche Hausaufgaben in Geschichte, Englisch und Biologie. Manchmal habe ich gar keine Zeit für meine Hobbys und meine Freunde.

**[Andreas]** Aber du hast doch am Wochenende Zeit, oder?

**[Mandy]** Normalerweise ja. Aber meine beste Freundin Nancy fährt oft mit ihren Eltern am Wochenende weg oder ist mit ihrem Tanzverein auf Tour, sodass ich sie nicht treffen kann. Und immer nur per Facebook oder Handy kommunizieren ist doch langweilig. Ich möchte lieber mit Nancy ins Kino gehen oder mal richtig shoppen. In der Woche habe ich dafür einfach keine Zeit.

**[Andreas]** Naja, du bist doch auch Mitglied in einem Sportverein – und gehst noch zur Musikschule. Ist das nicht zu viel?

**[Mandy]** Ich gehe sehr gern zum Gitarrenunterricht in die Musikschule, weil ich musikalisch bin und es mir sehr viel Spaß macht. Meine Lehrerin sagt, dass ich vielleicht bald in einem Konzert spielen kann. Und der Sportverein ist auch total wichtig für mich, weil ich meine Freunde dort habe. Ich liebe Leichtathletik – am liebsten sprinte ich. Ich kann mir nicht vorstellen, dass ich das aufgeben soll.

**[Andreas]** Und wie schaffst du das alles? Schule – Sportverein – Musikschule?

**[Mandy]** Jeden Sonntag mache ich einen Plan für die ganze Woche. Ich schreibe auf, was ich machen muss und bis wann ich das machen muss. Dann mache ich auch so viele Hausaufgaben wie möglich am Samstag und am Sonntag, damit die Woche nicht so voll ist. Und wenn ich Hilfe brauche, telefoniere ich mit meinen Freunden oder wir treffen uns vor der Schule und machen die Hausaufgaben zusammen. Aber manchmal ist das wirklich nicht so einfach …

**[Andreas]** Kann ich dir irgendwie helfen?

**[Mandy]** Oh ja, klasse. Mutti hat gesagt, dass ich abwaschen soll. Das ist aber super, dass du das für mich machst! Ich kann in der Zeit meine Englischvokabeln lernen.

**[Andreas]** Moment mal – ich meinte Hausaufgaben und nicht Hausarbeit!

**[Mandy]** Komm schon – Hilfe ist Hilfe. Du kannst sowieso ein bisschen mehr im Haushalt tun.

# Employability

## Monologue

*Markus talks about his experience of a job interview for a summer job.*

Es ist gar nicht so einfach einen Ferienjob für den Sommer zu finden. Sehr viele Studenten wollen in den Sommermonaten Geld verdienen, dann sind da noch die Schüler von den Gymnasien, die auch arbeiten wollen. Außerdem gibt es in meiner Heimatstadt nicht so viele Supermärkte und Geschäfte, wo man einen Teilzeitjob finden kann.

Aber ich hatte Glück – ich habe mich beworben und auch ein Vorstellungsgespräch bekommen. Meine Deutschlehrerin hat mir geholfen mich richtig vorzubereiten. Sie hat mir Tipps gegeben und mit mir die Fragen für das Interview diskutiert.

Meine Eltern sind mit mir einkaufen gegangen, damit ich die richtigen Klamotten für das Interview habe. Sie haben mir gesagt, was man in einem Supermarkt machen muss und dass man immer freundlich und höflich sein sollte.

Als ich dann zum Interview gegangen bin, war ich schon ein bisschen nervös. Aber die Personalmanagerin war sehr freundlich. Sie hat mir den Supermarkt gezeigt und mir gesagt, dass ich Regale füllen, sauber machen und an der Kasse arbeiten würde. Ich habe alle Fragen beantwortet und mich für das Interview bedankt.

Nach zwei Tagen hat mich die Personalmanagerin angerufen und mir gesagt, dass ich die Stelle habe. Nun werde ich in den Sommerferien arbeiten und mein eigenes Geld verdienen. Ich habe wirklich sehr viel Glück gehabt.

# Employability

## Dialogue

*Markus and Anita are talking about Anita's work experience.*

**[Markus]** Hallo, Anita, na – wie geht's? Und wie war dein Arbeitspraktikum?

**[Anita]** Oh, hallo Markus. Naja – es geht so. Ich bin total froh, dass mein Praktikum vorbei ist. Die Arbeit in einem Restaurant ist echt nichts für mich. Das ist mir alles viel zu hektisch. Manche Gäste sind sehr unfreundlich und der Koch war auch oft launisch.

**[Markus]** Was genau hast du im Restaurant gemacht?

**[Anita]** Naja, am ersten Tag habe ich die Tische sauber gemacht und in der Küche abgewaschen. Dann habe ich Getränke und Essen serviert und beim Kassieren geholfen.

**[Markus]** Wie bist du mit den anderen Kollegen ausgekommen?

**[Anita]** Wir waren ein gutes Team und haben einander geholfen – besonders wenn der Chef mal wieder schwierig war und schlechte Laune hatte. Mein Chef wollte immer, dass wir super schnell sind. Aber das ist gar nicht so einfach in einem großen Restaurant. Man muss sehr viel hin und her laufen und sehr viel tragen. Abends war ich oft totmüde.

**[Markus]** Und wie war der Kontakt mit den Gästen?

**[Anita]** Na, die meisten Gäste waren kein Problem – aber manchmal gab es Leute, die nicht mal fünf Minuten auf einen Kaffee warten konnten oder denen die Suppe zu kalt und das Essen zu heiß war. Schrecklich!

**[Markus]** Und was willst du in der Zukunft machen?

**[Anita]** Also auf keinen Fall werde ich in einem Restaurant arbeiten. Am liebsten würde ich mit Tieren im Zoo oder in einem Tierheim arbeiten. Ich interessiere mich auch für einen Beruf in der Landwirtschaft und würde gern mit Pferden oder mit anderen großen Tieren arbeiten.

**[Markus]** Denkst du, dass das Arbeitspraktikum eine gute Idee ist?

**[Anita]** Ja, auf jeden Fall. Man findet heraus, welcher der richtige Job ist und was man in diesem Job machen muss. Ich bin der Meinung, dass alle Schüler ein Arbeitspraktikum machen sollten und man sollte auch einen Teilzeitjob in den Ferien oder am Wochenende haben. Dann kann man Erfahrungen sammeln, die man später im Leben braucht.

**[Markus]** Stimmt. Na dann – viel Erfolg.

**[Anita]** Danke, dir auch.

# Culture

## Monologue

*Christine talks about her holiday plans.*

Im Mai werde ich 18 Jahre alt – und im Sommer kann ich dann endlich mit meinen Freunden in Urlaub fahren! Wir freuen uns schon sehr darauf, weil wir mehr Zeit miteinander verbringen können und all das machen werden, was Teenager gut finden.

Meine Freunde und ich haben vor, drei Wochen auf einem Campingplatz an der Ostsee Ferien zu machen. Der Campingplatz ist sehr modern, er liegt direkt am Strand und man kann dort auch surfen lernen und Strandvolleyball spielen. Es gibt außerdem einen kleinen Supermarkt und einen kleinen Golfplatz in der Nähe.

Wir wollen in den drei Wochen auch die großen Städte an der Ostsee kennen lernen. Rostock interessiert mich sehr, denn dort gibt es eine große Universität mit mehr als 14.000 Studenten. Man kann in Rostock Wassersport machen und mit der Fähre nach Dänemark oder Schweden fahren.

Urlaub mit meinen Eltern war manchmal ganz schön problematisch und anstrengend, denn sie haben ganz andere Interessen als ich und gehen sehr gern ins Museum und ins Restaurant. Ich aber bin sportlich und wünsche mir aktive Ferien.

Wenn man alleine ohne Eltern Ferien macht, wird man selbstständiger und man lernt alles genau zu planen und zu organisieren. Und wenn man ein Problem hat, muss man das selbst lösen. Ich denke, dass Urlaub mit Freunden eine gute Vorbereitung auf das Leben ist.

# Culture

## Dialogue

*Stefan and Christine talk about a long weekend in Berlin.*

[Christine] Sag mal, Stefan, ich habe gehört, dass du mit deinen Freunden ein langes Wochenende in Berlin planst?

[Stefan] Ja, das stimmt. Wir wollen in zwei Wochen für ein paar Tage nach Berlin fahren. Freitagnachmittag nehmen wir den Zug und kommen am Abend um 20 Uhr in Berlin an. Vom Bahnhof zum Hotel ist es nicht so weit, sodass wir entweder laufen oder mit dem Taxi fahren werden. Und am Montagabend kommen wir wieder zurück.

[Christine] Hast du die Reise organisiert?

[Stefan] Naja, nicht alleine natürlich. Aber ich habe die online Buchungen für das Hotel gemacht und auch die Fahrkarten online gekauft.

[Christine] Und wie sieht euer Programm für die vier Tage aus?

[Stefan] Am Samstag werden wir eine Stadtrundfahrt machen. Hoffentlich ist das Wetter gut, sodass wir in einem offenen Bus fahren können. Ich möchte sehr gern das Mauermuseum besuchen und auf den Fernsehturm fahren. Am Sonntag wollen wir in ein mexikanisches Restaurant am Potsdamer Platz gehen und einen Film im Sony Center sehen.

[Christine] Das hört sich gut an. Und was sagen deine Eltern dazu?

[Stefan] Meine Eltern sind sehr modern und verständnisvoll. Außerdem vertrauen sie mir. Meine Mutter ist der Meinung, dass man nur selbstständig wird, wenn man etwas alleine organisiert. Und meine Eltern haben keine Probleme mit meinen Freunden – sie kennen sie sehr gut.

[Christine] Wo würdest du gern einmal Ferien machen? Hast du ein Traumziel?

[Stefan] Naja, ich denke, das hat jeder. Ich würde sehr gern einmal in die Schweiz fahren, aber mein Traumziel ist die Stadt Sankt Petersburg in Russland. Aber man muss realistisch sein. Ferien kosten viel Geld und wenn man nicht mit den Eltern fahren will, muss man alles alleine bezahlen.

[Christine] Ja, das stimmt. Wie habt ihr denn das Geld für Berlin zusammen gekriegt?

[Stefan] Meine Freunde und ich haben Teilzeitjobs, sodass wir das Geld gespart haben. Naja, und ehrlich gesagt, meine Großeltern haben mir Geld zu Weihnachten geschenkt, damit ich die Berlin-Reise finanzieren kann.

[Christine] Na dann wünsche ich dir viel Spaß in der Hauptstadt. Schreib mal eine Postkarte.

[Stefan] Ich schicke dir eine Foto-SMS!

# Chapter 11

# Writing Course Assessment

This assessment counts for 20 marks. You will produce one written text, a job application in German, in response to a stimulus supported by six bullet points which you must address. See them as a checklist of information that you will have to provide in your response. **Four of the bullet points are predictable but two of them are less predictable as they vary from year to year.** The text you produce must take the form of an email and should be between 120 and 150 words in length. You may use a dictionary in this paper.

You must be able to demonstrate a sense of structure in your writing. You should also be aware that the level of accuracy in spelling and your command of German grammar (especially word order and verb endings) will have an influence on your writing grade. Make sure you address all six bullet points as you may have marks substracted if you miss one out.

At the end of this chapter you will find the SQA mark categories for writing. Study them carefully to understand in what way you can achieve the best grade.

> **Remember**
>
> The reading and writing part of the exam are both part of the same paper. You have a total of 1 hour and 30 minutes for both parts.

## Hints & tips

*Here are some tips to help you improve your grade:*

### Before you sit your writing exam

- ✓ *Plan the exam carefully by exploring the four predictable bullet points.*
- ✓ *Make sure you know the proper conventions for your piece of writing and practise them.*
- ✓ *Make a note of some vocabulary that you will need to address these bullet points and learn it. Choose five verbs, five adjectives and five nouns, for example.*
- ✓ *Remember what you have practised in class when covering the topic areas you are writing about.*
- ✓ *Produce a draft and show it to your teacher before the exam.*

### While you are sitting your writing exam

- ✓ *Read the stimulus very carefully and identify exactly what the job you are going to apply for is about. Use the dictionary for help if necessary and remember that jobs in German have male and female forms.*
- ✓ *Read the two bullet points which are less predictable. Remember what you have learned in class about the topics they address.*
- ✓ *Avoid writing very long sentences as you may lose control of structure and word order. However, try to include connectors such as* **und/aber/oder/denn** *and also some which change the word order such as* **weil/obwohl/dass.** ⇨

⇨

✓ *Try to use different tense forms where possible, e.g. "Ich habe im letzten Jahr ein Arbeitspraktikum gemacht."/"Ich werde das Abitur machen und Deutsch studieren."*

✓ *Where possible, include opinions using German expressions such as "Ich denke, dass …"/"Ich bin der Meinung, dass …"/"Ich finde …"/"Meiner Meinung nach …"*

✓ *Try not to translate from English as you will be tempted to apply the English sentence structure rather than the German one — focus on the correct position of the verb in the German sentence and remember the rules of German sentence structure.*

✓ *Limit yourself to 20–25 words per bullet point and make sure you address them all.*

✓ *Focus on capitalisation of nouns and correct verb endings to achieve a high level of accuracy.*

## After you have finished your writing exam

✓ *Leave yourself enough time at the end to proofread your email text.*

✓ *Check that you have addressed all six bullet points.*

✓ *Check your verb endings and tense forms, your adjective endings and capitalisation of nouns.*

✓ *If in doubt, use the dictionary for support.*

Here is a writing task for you to practise on.

### Task

You are preparing an application for the job advertised below and you write an email to the company in German.

---

**Hotel Adlon Kempinski in Berlin – wo Stars und Sternchen zu Hause sind**

Das Luxushotel Adlon am Brandenburger Tor in Berlin sucht Personal für die folgenden Bereiche:

● Hotelrezeption
● Zimmerservice
● Restaurant
● Küchenassistenz

Sie sollten höflich, freundlich, motiviert und diskret sein sowie sehr gute Deutsch– und Englischkenntnisse haben.

Wenn Sie motiviert sind und selbstständig arbeiten können, bewerben Sie sich per E-mail: hotel.adlon@kempinski.com

# Planning your answer

To help you write your email, you have been given the following checklist of information to offer about yourself and to ask about the job. You must include all of these points:

- personal details (name, age, where you live)
- school/college/education experience until now
- skills/interests you have which make you right for the job
- related work experience
- reasons for applying
- your experience of travelling in other countries.

The email should be approximately 120–150 words. You may use a German dictionary. Try to approach the task logically, following Steps 1–4 below.

### Remember

The first four bullet points are the same every year. They are predictable. You can prepare them in class with the help of your teacher. The last two bullet points vary within reason. You will be able to tackle them successfully if you apply your knowledge of German grammar and vocabulary.

## Step 1

The first four bullet points cover topic areas you have dealt with in your German coursework. Find your notes and handouts on these to support your writing.

- **Personal details**

  *Ich heiße Christopher Bell und ich bin 17 Jahre alt. Seit meiner Geburt wohne ich in Glasgow an der Westküste von Schottland. (22 words)*

- **School/college/education experience until now**

  *Seit fünf Jahren besuche ich eine Gesamtschule in der Stadtmitte von Glasgow. Ich bin ein sehr guter Schüler und ich werde im nächsten Jahr das Abitur machen. Deutsch und Geschichte sind meine Lieblingsfächer. (33 words)*

- **Skills/interests you have which make you right for the job**

  *Ich interessiere mich sehr für Fremdsprachen. Außerdem kann ich gut mit Menschen umgehen, weil ich freundlich und höflich bin. Meine Lehrer sind der Meinung, dass ich eine positive Lernhaltung habe. (30 words)*

- **Related work experience**

  *Im letzten Jahr habe ich ein Arbeitspraktikum in einem internationalen Hotel in Glasgow gemacht. Dort habe ich an der Rezeption gearbeitet. Die Arbeit hat mir sehr viel Spaß gemacht. (29 words)*

The last two bullet points will be unpredictable. Here are suggestions:

- **Reasons for applying**

  *Ich würde sehr gern in Deutschland arbeiten, sodass ich das Land und die Kultur besser kennen lernen kann. Dann möchte ich auch meine Deutschkenntnisse verbessern. (25 words)*

- **Your experience of travelling in other countries**

  *Vor zwei Monaten war ich mit meiner Klasse in Holland. Die Reise hat mir sehr gut gefallen, weil ich das erste Mal in Holland war. Andere Länder und Kulturen faszinieren mich. (31 words)*

**Total word count:** 170 words

You can see that even with very short responses to each bullet point, it is quite easy to achieve the total word count of 120–150 words. You will not be penalised if you exceed this word count, but it won't give you an advantage.

## Step 2

Make sure that you prepare yourself thoroughly. Give yourself plenty of time to learn the German you need for the first four bullet points. You might want to use them as part of your talking assessment which will save you extra work.

## Step 3

Revise the following features of German grammar: word order, present tense (verb endings), perfect tense expressing past, adjective endings before nouns, dative case, accusative case.

## Step 4

Practise possible scenarios for the two unpredictable bullet points. Here are some ideas that might come up:
- when you will be available for interview and to work
- your experience of working with the public
- languages spoken
- your specific language skills
- reason(s) for wanting to work in Germany
- which games, sports and activities you could help organise
- your experience of working with young people
- previous contacts with Germany
- your experience of working at functions or events.

*Remember*

The most important things are structure and accuracy!

## Remember

The positive aspect of the Writing Course Assessment is that you are in control of the preparation. Make a big effort, ask your teacher for help and you can't go wrong.

To help you further, the SQA marking grid for the Writing Course Assessment is reproduced below. It explains clearly why a particular mark is awarded and what criteria have been met (or missed) to obtain the mark.

| Category | Mark | Content | Accuracy | Language resource – variety, range, structures |
|---|---|---|---|---|
| Very good | 20 | The job advert has been addressed in a full and balanced way. The candidate uses detailed language.<br><br>The candidate addresses the advert completely and competently, including information in response to both unpredictable bullet points.<br><br>A range of verbs/verb forms, tenses and constructions is used.<br><br>Overall this comes over as a competent, well thought-out and serious application for the job. | The candidate handles all aspects of grammar and spelling accurately, although the language may contain one or two minor errors.<br><br>Where the candidate attempts to use language more appropriate to Higher, a slightly higher number of inaccuracies need not detract from the overall very good impression. | The candidate is comfortable with the first person of the verb and generally uses a different verb in each sentence.<br><br>Some modal verbs and infinitives may be used.<br><br>There is good use of adjectives, adverbs and prepositional phrases and, where appropriate, word order. There may be a range of tenses.<br><br>The candidate uses co-ordinating conjunctions and/or subordinate clauses where appropriate.<br><br>The language of the email flows well. |
| Good | 16 | The job advert has been addressed competently.<br><br>There is less evidence of detailed language.<br><br>The candidate uses a reasonable range of verbs/verb forms.<br><br>Overall, the candidate has produced a genuine, reasonably accurate attempt at applying for the specific job, even though he/she may not address one of the unpredictable bullet points. | The candidate handles a range of verbs fairly accurately.<br><br>There are some errors in spelling, adjective endings and, where relevant, case endings. Use of accents is less secure, where appropriate.<br><br>Where the candidate is attempting to use more complex vocabulary and structures, these may be less successful, although basic structures are used accurately.<br><br>There may be one or two examples of inaccurate dictionary use, especially in the unpredictable bullet points. | There may be repetition of verbs.<br><br>There may be examples of listing, in particular when referring to school/college experience, without further amplification.<br><br>There may be one or two examples of a co-ordinating conjunction, but most sentences are simple sentences.<br><br>The candidate keeps to more basic vocabulary, particularly in response to either or both unpredictable bullet points. |

| Satisfactory | 12 | The job advert has been addressed fairly competently. | The verbs are generally correct, but may be repetitive. | The candidate copes with the first and third person of a few verbs, where appropriate. |
|---|---|---|---|---|
| | | The candidate makes limited use of detailed language. | There are quite a few errors in other parts of speech — gender of nouns, cases, singular/plural confusion, for instance. | A limited range of verbs is used. |
| | | The language is fairly repetitive and uses a limited range of verbs and fixed phrases, e.g. *I like, I go, I play*. | | Sentences are basic and mainly brief. |
| | | The candidate copes fairly well with areas of personal details, education, skills, interests and work experience but does not deal fully with the two unpredictable bullet points and indeed may not address either or both of the unpredictable bullet points. | Prepositions may be missing, e.g. *I go the town*. | There is minimal use of adjectives, probably mainly after 'is', e.g. *Chemistry is interesting*. |
| | | | Overall, there is more correct than incorrect. | The candidate has a weak knowledge of plurals. |
| | | On balance, however, the candidate has produced a satisfactory job application in the specific language. | | There may be several spelling errors, e.g. reversal of vowel combinations. |
| Unsatisfactory | 8 | The job advert has been addressed in an uneven manner and/or with insufficient use of detailed language. | Ability to form tenses is inconsistent. | The candidate copes mainly only with the personal language required in bullet points 1 and 2. |
| | | The language is repetitive, e.g. *I like, I go, I play* may feature several times. | There are errors in many other parts of speech — gender of nouns, cases, singular/plural confusion, for instance. | The verbs 'is' and 'study' may also be used correctly. |
| | | There may be little difference between Satisfactory and Unsatisfactory. | Several errors are serious, perhaps showing mother tongue interference. | Sentences are basic. |
| | | **Either or both of the unpredictable bullet points may not have been addressed.** | The detail in the unpredictable bullet points may be very weak. | An English word may appear in the writing. |
| | | There may be one sentence which is not intelligible to a sympathetic native speaker. | Overall, there is more incorrect than correct. | There may be an example of serious dictionary misuse. |
| Poor | 4 | The candidate has had considerable difficulty in addressing the job advert. There is little evidence of the use of detailed language. | Many of the verbs are incorrect. | The candidate cannot cope with more than one or two basic verbs. |
| | | Three or four sentences may not be understood by a sympathetic native speaker. | There are many errors in other parts of speech — personal pronouns, gender of nouns, cases, singular/plural confusion, prepositions, for instance. | The candidate displays almost no knowledge of the present tense of verbs. |
| | | **Either or both of the unpredictable bullet points may not have been addressed.** | The language is probably inaccurate throughout the writing. | Verbs used more than once may be written differently on each occasion. |
| | | | | Sentences are very short. |
| | | | | The candidate has a very limited vocabulary. |
| | | | | Several English words may appear in the writing. |
| | | | | There are examples of serious dictionary misuse. |

| Very poor | 0 | The candidate is unable to address the job advert.<br><br>**The two unpredictable bullet points may not have been addressed.**<br><br>Very little is intelligible to a sympathetic native speaker. | Virtually nothing is correct. | The candidate may only cope with the verbs 'to have' and 'to be'.<br><br>Very few words are written correctly in the modern language.<br><br>English words are used.<br><br>There may be several examples of mother tongue interference.<br><br>There may be several examples of serious dictionary misuse. |
|---|---|---|---|---|

# Chapter 12

# Talking Course Assessment

This assessment counts for 30 marks. The Performance Talking Assessment will be carried out in your school by your German teacher who will be able to help you to prepare for it well in advance. It will be recorded and marked by your teacher. It is possible for you to 'recycle' your Talking Unit Assessment (Using Language Unit) for the Course Assessment. The Performance Talking Assessment has two parts:

1   A presentation in German on a topic of your choice, such as:
    ● *Meine Familie und ich*
    ● *Meine Freizeit und meine Freunde*
    ● *Meine Heimatstadt*
    ● *Meine Schule und meine Schulkarriere*
    ● *Meine Zukunftspläne*
    ● *Mein Arbeitspraktikum*
    ● *Mein Lieblingsfilm*
    ● *Mein Lieblingsbuch*

    The presentation should be approximately two to three minutes long. You may use notes (not sentences) and/or visual support such as a PowerPoint presentation, a picture, a photograph, an item, etc.

2   A discussion with your teacher in German:
    Your teacher will ask you additional questions on your presentation or may ask questions which relate to a topic derived from your presentation. The discussion should be approximately three to five minutes long.

The total mark for your speaking exam at National 5 is 30. Five out of these 30 marks will only be granted if the language you use in the conversation is natural and spontaneous.

How can you achieve these five marks? Most importantly, you should try to sustain the conversation. Do not give up if you don't understand a question your teacher asks you. Use sentences like "*Wie bitte?*" or "*Können Sie das bitte wiederholen?*" to signal to your teacher that you need clarification. Be sure that your teacher won't let you down.

Also, take the initiative and ask your teacher questions, too. Remember to use *Sie* in German when you talk to an adult who is not a member of your family.

## Check this out !

| | |
|---|---|
| Hast du eine große oder eine kleine Familie? | Haben Sie eine große oder kleine Familie? |
| Was machst du in deiner Freizeit? | Was machen Sie in Ihrer Freizeit? |
| Siehst du gern Filme im Fernsehen? | Sehen Sie gern Filme im Fernsehen? |
| Warum ist dein Handy wichtig für dich? | Warum ist Ihr Handy wichtig für Sie? |

⇨

| Wie findest du deine Schule? | Wie finden Sie Ihre Schule? |
| --- | --- |
| Was möchtest du in der Zukunft machen? | Was möchten Sie in der Zukunft machen? |
| Hast du ein Arbeitspraktikum gemacht? | Haben Sie als Schüler/Schülerin ein Arbeitspraktikum gemacht? |
| Warum gefällt dir Deutsch? | Warum gefällt Ihnen Deutsch? |
| Warst du schon einmal in Deutschland? | Waren Sie schon einmal in Deutschland? |
| Hast du ein Traumreiseziel? | Haben Sie ein Traumreiseziel? |

## Hints & tips ⭐

### Talking tips to improve your grade

✓ *Start preparing for your speaking exam in plenty of time. Practise speaking regularly as practice makes perfect.*

✓ *Remember that your teacher will conduct the exam and that he/she will want to help you to succeed. Trust him/her.*

### Before your speaking exam

✓ *Choose a topic that you really like and have something to say about for your presentation.*

✓ *Develop a piece of writing for your presentation which has a clear structure. Show this work to your teacher.*

✓ *Ask your teacher to read aloud and record this text for you on your mobile phone, iPod or any other media device so that you can listen to it many times before the exam.*

✓ *Turn the sentences of that text into notes. (A note is a short phrase which does not contain a verb.)*

✓ *Practise your presentation by listening to the recording and reading your notes, then try it without the recording by your teacher.*

✓ *Try to figure out what kind of questions your teacher might ask you in the discussion. These questions will be linked to the topic you have presented. If you have done a presentation on your favourite film, your teacher might ask questions such as these:*

*"Siehst du gern fern oder gehst du lieber ins Kino?"*

*"Was findest du besser — DVDs zu Hause oder einen Kinofilm mit Freunden sehen?"*

*"Welche Filme siehst du gern?"*

*"Welche Fernsehsendungen siehst du gern?"*

*Make sure you revise and learn the conventions on expressing an opinion in German, e.g. "Ich finde …", "Ich bin der Meinung, dass …", "Meiner Meinung nach …", etc.*

*You should also revise and learn conventions on how to sustain a conversation — especially when you have difficulties understanding a question, e.g. "Ich habe das nicht verstanden. Bitte wiederholen Sie die Frage."/"Ich bin nicht sicher, was das auf Deutsch/Englisch heißt."/"Sprechen Sie bitte langsamer."*

## During your speaking exam

✓ *Concentrate on your notes in your presentation. You are entitled to use them – do not do without.*

✓ *Look up from your notes, keep eye contact and speak loudly and clearly to show you are confident – and to ensure a good quality of recording!*

✓ *Do not panic if you are stuck – try to recover by remembering what you have worked out for your presentation.*

✓ *Listen carefully to your teacher's questions and remember that you can always 'steal' vocabulary from the question to make your answer.*

✓ *Try to avoid very long sentences as you might lose control over the sentence structure. However, try to use connectors such as **und/aber/oder/denn** and also **weil**.*

✓ *Ask for help in German when you need it. This will not necessarily result in a lower mark as it shows your ability to use German for clarification purposes.*

## After your speaking exam

✓ *Ask your teacher if it is possible to listen to your recording and get some feedback on your performance.*

✓ *You might want to use your National 5 speaking exam as a basis for your Higher speaking exam – so keep your notes if you are thinking about taking Higher German.*

### Check this out !

In your National 5 Course Assessment, the formula for success is a sound knowledge of the level of German required, teamwork in class and with your teacher, and confidence in yourself and the skills your teacher has helped you to develop. Most importantly though, enjoy your German classes, as well as the course and the experience.

*Deutsch ist mega cool!*

In order to do some authentic N5 German Course Assessment practice, please look at Hodder Gibson's *SQA Specimen Paper, 2014 Past Paper National 5 German & Hodder Gibson Model Papers.*

To help you further, the SQA marking grids for the Talking Course Assessment are reproduced below. They explain clearly the criteria within each of the three 'specific commentary' areas – **presentation**, **conversation** and **conversation-natural element** – and what you should aim to include/achieve in order to be awarded a particular mark, as well as outlining possible problem areas when marks at the lower end are given.

| Categories | Specific commentary<br>Presentation | Pegged marks |
|---|---|---|
| Very good | <ul><li>Speaks fluently and without undue hesitation, and/or recovers well when there is some hesitation.</li><li>A wide range of vocabulary and structures appropriate to National 5.</li><li>Handles most aspects of grammar accurately, although there may be some minor errors.</li><li>Pronunciation and intonation sufficient to be readily understood by a sympathetic speaker of the language.</li></ul> | 10 |
| Good | <ul><li>May speak with some degree of hesitation, but generally recovers well.</li><li>An appropriate range of vocabulary and structures for National 5.</li><li>Pronunciation and intonation sufficient to be generally understood by a sympathetic speaker of the language.</li></ul> | 8 |
| Satisfactory | <ul><li>Handles language appropriate to National 5 with a degree of grammatical accuracy sufficient to ensure that communication is achieved.</li><li>May speak with a considerable degree of hesitation, but makes some attempt to recover.</li><li>Pronunciation and intonation sufficient to be understood by a sympathetic speaker of the language.</li></ul> | 6 |
| Unsatisfactory | <ul><li>Difficulty in achieving communication because of limited range of vocabulary and structures and/or serious inaccuracies in language appropriate to National 5.</li><li>May speak with considerable degree of hesitation, but makes some attempt to recover.</li><li>Pronunciation and intonation sufficient to be understood by a sympathetic speaker of the language, although some points may not be immediately clear.</li></ul> | 4 |
| Poor | <ul><li>Communication seriously impeded because of limited range of vocabulary and structures and/or serious inaccuracies in language appropriate to National 5.</li><li>Pronunciation and/or intonation may be such as would not be readily understood without clarification, even by a sympathetic speaker of the language.</li></ul> | 2 |
| Very poor | <ul><li>Very little is intelligible to a sympathetic speaker of the language.</li></ul> | 0 |

| Categories | Specific commentary | Pegged marks |
|---|---|---|
| | Conversation | |
| Very good | <ul><li>Understands almost all of what is said.</li><li>The interlocutor can speak at normal speed, using detailed language, occasionally using repetition and/or rephrasing.</li><li>Can respond using detailed language to express a wide range of ideas and opinions.</li><li>Can sustain the conversation by, for example, asking relevant questions and by seeking help when necessary.</li></ul> | 15 |
| Good | <ul><li>Understands most of what is said, although may require some clarification.</li><li>The interlocutor can usually speak at normal speed, using a range of detailed language, using repetition and/or rephrasing when required.</li><li>The interlocutor may have to provide some help or prompting.</li><li>Can respond using some detailed language to express some ideas and opinions.</li><li>Can sustain the conversation by, for example, asking relevant questions and by seeking help when necessary.</li></ul> | 12 |
| Satisfactory | <ul><li>Understands some of what is said, although may require some clarification.</li><li>The interlocutor can occasionally use a range of detailed language.</li><li>The interlocutor can sometimes speak at normal speed, and frequently uses repetition and/or rephrasing.</li><li>The interlocutor may have to provide help and prompting frequently.</li><li>Can respond with some ideas and opinions.</li><li>Can use some limited familiar detailed language.</li><li>May attempt to sustain the conversation by, for example, asking relevant questions and by seeking help when necessary.</li></ul> | 9 |
| Unsatisfactory (near miss) | <ul><li>Has difficulty in understanding what is said, even with help.</li><li>The interlocutor can only use familiar detailed language.</li><li>The interlocutor speaks slowly and uses repetition and re-phrasing frequently.</li><li>The interlocutor may have to provide help with every question.</li><li>Responds with minimal ideas and opinions.</li><li>Has difficulty in sustaining the conversation.</li></ul> | 6 |
| Poor | <ul><li>Has difficulty in understanding most of what is said.</li><li>The interlocutor can only use a limited range of familiar detailed language.</li><li>The interlocutor speaks slowly and has to use repetition and re-phrasing for most questions.</li><li>The interlocutor has to provide help with every question.</li><li>May frequently respond with one-word answers.</li><li>Cannot sustain the conversation.</li></ul> | 3 |
| Very poor | <ul><li>Understands very little of what is said despite repetition and rephrasing.</li><li>Very little is intelligible to a sympathetic speaker of the language.</li></ul> | 0 |

| Categories | Specific commentary | Pegged marks |
|---|---|---|
| | Conversation – natural element | |
| Very good | The candidate is able to sustain and maintain a natural conversation, responding to some questions and employing a range of techniques. | 5 |
| Satisfactory | The candidate can, with help and prompting, adequately maintain a natural conversation and respond to some questions. | 3 |
| Very poor | The candidate is unable to sustain or maintain a conversation and cannot go beyond the use of learned material. | 0 |

# Chapter 13

# Practice activities

The activities in this chapter should help you to strengthen your understanding of National 5 German vocabulary and grammar, and cover typical aspects of German language that you will encounter at National 5. It is essential for you to revise systematically before your exam. Use your coursework material in the first instance and any other help sheets or resources which your German teacher might give you. Make sure you have a good dictionary and you know how to use it effectively.

The following activities should help you to revise according to the contexts in National 5 (Society, Learning, Employability, Culture). Although the tasks are only a selection of what is in the course, they should support your revision significantly and give you more confidence in understanding the logic behind German. Each activity has a stopwatch icon to let you know how long you have to complete it. Let's start.

*Los geht's!*

# Society

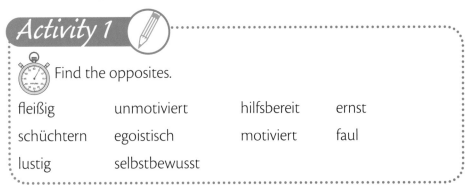

**Activity 1**

Find the opposites.

| fleißig | unmotiviert | hilfsbereit | ernst |
| schüchtern | egoistisch | motiviert | faul |
| lustig | selbstbewusst | | |

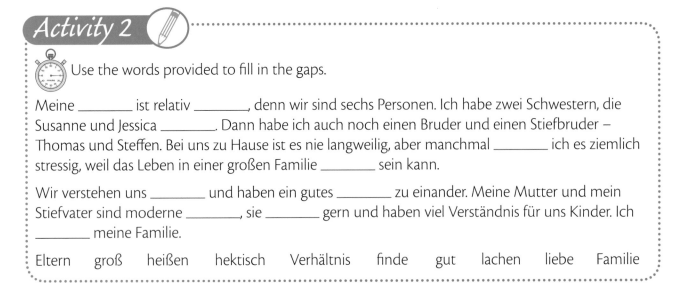

**Activity 2**

Use the words provided to fill in the gaps.

Meine _____ ist relativ _____, denn wir sind sechs Personen. Ich habe zwei Schwestern, die Susanne und Jessica _____. Dann habe ich auch noch einen Bruder und einen Stiefbruder – Thomas und Steffen. Bei uns zu Hause ist es nie langweilig, aber manchmal _____ ich es ziemlich stressig, weil das Leben in einer großen Familie _____ sein kann.

Wir verstehen uns _____ und haben ein gutes _____ zu einander. Meine Mutter und mein Stiefvater sind moderne _____, sie _____ gern und haben viel Verständnis für uns Kinder. Ich _____ meine Familie.

Eltern     groß     heißen     hektisch     Verhältnis     finde     gut     lachen     liebe     Familie

## Activity 3

 Complete the sentences with the correct form of the verb in the present tense.

1  Tom _____ eine relativ große Familie. (haben)
2  Seine Eltern, seine drei Brüder und er _____ in einem Bauernhaus auf dem Land. (wohnen)
3  Das Haus _____ sehr groß aber auch sehr alt. (sein)
4  Jeden Tag _____ Tom im Haushalt. (helfen)
5  Er _____ mit dem Hund spazieren und _____ den Müll raus. (gehen, bringen)
6  In seiner Freizeit _____ er sehr gern Computerspiele und Fußball. (spielen)
7  Was _____ du in deiner Freizeit? (machen)

## Activity 4

### Freunde und Freundschaft

Read the following four statements. Find the German for the English words and phrases given underneath each paragraph.

#### Jessica

Meine Freunde sind super wichtig für mich, denn ich bin ein Einzelkind und habe eine relativ kleine Familie. Mein Freundeskreis ist sehr groß, aber meine beste Freundin heißt Steffi. Wir kommen gut miteinander aus, obwohl Steffi manchmal ein bisschen launisch ist. Freunde sollten hilfsbereit und verständnisvoll sein.

*very important      a rather small family      my circle of friends*
*We get on well with each other      helpful and understanding*

#### Thomas

Ich habe einen kleinen Freundeskreis, aber die meisten Freunde kenne ich schon sehr lange. Wir sind zusammen in die Grundschule gegangen und waren im gleichen Sportverein. Seit einem Jahr habe ich eine Freundin – Anja. Ich finde sie sehr attraktiv, weil sie lange, blonde Haare hat und das hübscheste Lächeln der Welt. Außerdem spielt sie Fußball und interessiert sich sehr für Sport. Anja ist mir sehr wichtig.

*most friends      together      girlfriend*
*the prettiest smile in the world      moreover*

#### Bernd

Meine Familie ist wichtiger als meine Freunde. Ich komme aus einer sehr großen Familie und ich habe vier Geschwister. Wir leben auf einem Bauernhof auf dem Land. Meiner Meinung nach ist es toll, ⇨

⇨

so viele Leute im Haus zu haben. Meine Großeltern wohnen auch bei uns; sie helfen im Haushalt, im Stall und im Garten. Wir haben eine große Landwirtschaft mit 500 Kühen.

*more important than*     *four siblings*     *on a farm*
*in the country*     *in the household*

**Susi**

Meine Eltern sind ständig unterwegs. Meine Mutter leitet eine Bank und mein Vater arbeitet als Chefarzt in einem großen Krankenhaus. Geschwister habe ich nicht und ich besuche eine Internatsschule. Dort ist es wie in einer Familie. Die Lehrer wohnen auf dem Campus und es ist immer jemand da, wenn man reden möchte oder ein Problem hat. Meine Freunde gehen alle in meine Schule. Ihre Eltern arbeiten auch sehr viel, sodass sie selten nach Hause fahren. Das gleiche Schicksal verbindet.

*constantly away*     *senior consultant*     *I attend a boarding*
*their parents*     *if you want to talk*     *school*

## Das erste Date – was tun?

1   Here is a checklist on how to prepare for a first date. Which of these statements offer valuable advice? Tick the box that you feel is most appropriate.

| Wie sollte man sich auf das erste Date vorbereiten? | Das würde ich machen. | Das würde ich nicht machen. |
|---|---|---|
| Man sollte mit seinem besten Freund oder seiner besten Freundin darüber reden. | | |
| Man sollte mit seinen Eltern darüber reden. | | |
| Man sollte das erste Date auf den Facebook-Status auf die Pinwand posten. | | |
| Man sollte ins Kino gehen und in der letzten Reihe sitzen. | | |
| Man sollte in ein Café in der Stadtmitte gehen. | | |
| Man sollte coole Klamotten tragen. | | |
| Man sollte Aftershave oder Parfüm tragen. | | |
| Man sollte den kleinen Bruder oder die kleine Schwester mitnehmen. | | |
| Man sollte den älteren Bruder oder die ältere Schwester mitnehmen. | | |
| Man sollte das Mobiltelefon zu Hause lassen. | | |

⇨

⇨

**2** Now make five sentences using *würde* or *würde nicht* to say what you would or would not do on your first date.

**Example:** Ich würde mit meinen Eltern darüber sprechen. Ich würde nicht das erste Date auf den Facebook-Status auf die Pinwand posten.

## Activity 6

### Was für ein Spiel ist das?

Match the hobby to the description.

**1** Zehn Spieler sind auf dem Feld und einer steht im Tor. Man braucht für dieses Spiel einen Ball.

**2** Zwei Spieler schlagen einen kleinen, relativ harten Ball über ein Netz.

**3** Für diesen Sport braucht man ein Hallenbad oder ein Freibad, wenn die Sonne scheint.

**4** Dieses Hobby ist ein Nationalsport in Schottland. Man muss einen kleinen, sehr harten Ball sehr weit schlagen und dann vorsichtig einlochen.

**5** Für dieses Hobby braucht man eine Kamera.

**6** Bücher, Zeitschriften, Zeitungen, ein Kindle – das braucht man für dieses Hobby.

**7** Wenn man musikalisch ist, sollte man dieses Hobby haben.

**8** Wenn man kreativ ist, dann hat man meistens dieses Hobby.

**9** Die neuen Medien machen dieses Hobby möglich.

**10** Es ist ein Brettspiel mit weißen und schwarzen Steinen. Man muss logisch denken, wenn man es spielt.

| | | |
|---|---|---|
| *Golf* | *Schach* | *ein Instrument spielen* |
| *Fußball* | *Fotografieren* | *Schwimmen*    *Lesen* |
| *im Internet surfen* | *Tennis* | *Zeichnen* |

## Activity 7

### Weil

Join the following sentences. Use *weil* and remember that 'the verb runs a mile'. Once you're done that, translate the sentences into English.

**1** Man sollte viel Wasser trinken. Der Körper muss hydriert sein.

**2** Meine Mutter isst keine Schokolade. Schokolade hat zu viel Zucker und Fett.

**3** Mein Vati raucht nicht mehr. Er will gesünder leben.

**4** Jeden Tag esse ich Obst und Gemüse. Das hat fast keine Kalorien.

**5** Drogen sind ein großes Problem für Jugendliche. Sie können süchtig werden.

⇨

⇨

6  Alkohol ist die gefährlichste Droge. Man kann überall Alkohol kaufen.

7  Ich rauche nicht. Die Klamotten stinken und es kostet zu viel Geld.

8  Meine Schwester joggt jeden Morgen durch den Park. Sie will fit bleiben.

9  Mein bester Freund hat eine Medaille im Schwimmen gewonnen. Er hat immer hart trainiert.

10  Nächstes Jahr werde ich einen Halbmarathon laufen. Ich möchte Geld für ein Kinderkrankenhaus sammeln und spenden.

## Neue Medien

a)  Put the following words and phrases into the correct category.

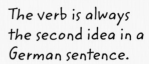

**Remember**

The verb is always the second idea in a German sentence.

| | das Fernsehen | das Internet | das Handy |
|---|---|---|---|
| einen Breitbandanschluss haben | | | |
| ein Kinderprogramm sehen | | | |
| mit Freunden chatten | | | |
| abends surfen | | | |
| ab und zu mailen | | | |
| regelmäßig skypen | | | |
| einen preiswerten Vertrag haben | | | |
| ein Facebook-Profil haben | | | |
| keinen Lieblingsfilm haben | | | |
| Seifenopern langweilig finden | | | |
| Talentshows peinlich finden | | | |
| eine Twitter-Funktion haben | | | |
| Fotos machen können | | | |
| einen eigenen Fernseher mit DVD-Spieler haben | | | |
| kurze Videos machen können | | | |

b)  Rewrite the following sentences. Start with the underlined phrase.

1  Wir haben <u>seit drei Jahren</u> einen Breitbandanschluss zu Hause.

2  Meine Oma sieht <u>jeden Abend</u> das Kinderprogramm mit meinem kleinen Bruder.

3  Ich chatte <u>am Wochenende</u> den ganzen Tag mit meinen Freunden.

4  Meine Mutter surft <u>abends</u> im Internet.

5  Meine Tante mailt <u>ab und zu</u> Fotos aus Amerika.

6  Ich kann regelmäßig <u>mit meinen Freunden</u> in Deutschland skypen.   ⇨

⇨

  7  Meine Eltern haben <u>endlich</u> einen preiswerten Vertrag für Telefon und Internet.

  8  Meine Katze hat <u>seit einer Woche</u> ein Facebook-Profil!

  9  Meine Freundin hat <u>meiner Meinung nach</u> keinen Lieblingsfilm.

10  Mein Opa findet Seifenopern <u>sehr oft</u> langweilig.

11  Ich finde Talentshows <u>jedesmal</u> peinlich.

12  Sabines Handy hat <u>mit Sicherheit</u> eine Twitter-Funktion.

13  Ich kann <u>im Urlaub</u> mit meinem neuen Handy Fotos machen.

14  Mein Bruder möchte <u>zu Weihnachten</u> einen eigenen Fernseher mit DVD-Spieler haben.

15  Thomas kann mit seiner Kamera <u>ohne Probleme</u> kurze Videos machen.

| my home town | *meine Heimatstadt* |
|---|---|

## Meine Heimatstadt

**a)** Complete the sentences with the correct word for 'a/an' in German. Remember: there are three choices – *einen, eine, ein*.

1  Meine Heimatstadt hat _____ Rathaus in der Stadtmitte. (das)

2  In der Stadt gibt es _____ Supermarkt neben der Post. (der)

3  Meine Heimatstadt hat _____ Schule mit etwa 500 Schülern. (die)

4  Es gibt auch _____ Museum und _____ Burg. (das, die)

5  In der Stadt findet man _____ Einkaufszentrum mit vielen Geschäften. (das)

6  Es gibt _____ Bahnhof und _____ Flughafen. (der, der)

7  Meine Heimatstadt hat _____ Schwimmhalle sowie _____ Fitnessstudio. (die, das)

8  Es gibt auch _____ Golfplatz und _____ Fußballstadion. (der, das)

**b)** Complete the sentences with the correct form of *einen, eine* or *ein* and add the correct ending to the adjective.

1  Meine Heimatstadt hat _____ Rathaus in der Stadtmitte. (das, historisch)

2  In der Stadt gibt es _____ Supermarkt neben der Post. (der, modern)  ⇨

⇨

3  Meine Heimatstadt hat _____ Schule mit etwa 500 Schülern. (die, sehr gut)

4  Es gibt auch _____ Museum und _____ Burg. (das, interessant) (die, mittelalterlich)

5  In der Stadt findet man _____ Einkaufszentrum mit vielen Geschäften. (das, groß)

6  Es gibt _____ Bahnhof und _____ Flughafen. (der, klein) (der, international)

7  Meine Heimatstadt hat _____ Schwimmhalle sowie _____ Fitnessstudio. (die, toll) (das, preiswert)

8  Es gibt auch _____ Golfplatz und _____ Fußballstadion. (der, klein) (das, traditionell)

## Activity 10

 Ich wohne gern hier

Read the following statements. Decide whether the person likes living in their home town or not. Give a reason for your answer.

1  Ich finde meine Heimatstadt zu klein und total langweilig, denn es gibt hier nichts für Jugendliche.

2  Meine Stadt hat keinen Bahnhof und keine Universität, sodass alle jungen Leute nach der Schule weggehen – das finde ich frustrierend.

3  Ich denke, dass meine Heimatstadt toll ist, weil die Einwohner freundlich und hilfsbereit sind.

4  Ich wohne gern hier, weil ich meine Familie und meine Freunde hier habe.

5  Ich möchte ganz schnell wegziehen, denn ich finde das Leben in einer Großstadt viel interessanter.

6  Ich wohne in Edinburgh – das ist die beste Stadt der Welt!

7  Später möchte ich in meiner Heimatstadt wohnen – es ist nirgends so schön wie zu Hause!

# Learning

## Activity 1

 Deine Schule

Match the questions and answers below.

1 Wie heißt deine Schule?
2 Was für eine Schule ist das?
3 Wann beginnt und wann endet dein Schultag?
4 Wie viele Stunden pro Tag hast du?
5 Wie lang ist die Mittagspause?
6 Hast du ein Lieblingsfach?
7 Welches Fach gefällt dir nicht?
8 Hast du eine Schuluniform?
9 Welche Klubs gibt es in deiner Schule?
10 Seit wann lernst du Deutsch?

a) Mein Schultag beginnt um neun Uhr und endet um halb Vier.
b) Ja, ich trage eine schwarze Hose, ein weißes Hemd und eine Schulkrawatte. Wir haben auch schwarze Schulblazer.
c) Meine Schule heißt Langholm Academy.
d) Die Mittagspause ist 50 Minuten lang.
e) Mathe gefällt mir gar nicht, weil es total schwierig ist.
f) Langholm Academy ist eine Gesamtschule und Ganztagsschule.
g) Mein Lieblingsfach ist Musik, weil ich musikalisch bin und Klavier spiele.
h) Die Schule hat viele Sportklubs, ein Schulorchester und einen Hausaufgabenklub.
i) Wir haben sieben Stunden pro Tag.
j) Ich lerne seit drei Jahren Deutsch.

## Activity 2

Weil und denn

Join the sentences using the connector in brackets.

1 Ich mag meine Schule. Die Lehrer haben Zeit für die Schüler. (weil)
2 In der Schulkantine kann man etwas Warmes essen. Die Köchinnen kochen jeden Tag selbst. (denn)
3 Wir können Hausaufgaben in der Schule machen. Wir haben eine Schulbibliothek. (denn)
4 Ich finde meine Schule sehr modern. Es gibt sehr viele Computer. (weil)
5 Die Lehrer sparen Papier. Jedes Klassenzimmer hat einen Computer und eine elektronische Tafel. (weil)
6 Ich gehe gern in die Schule. Ich bin neugierig und lerne gern. (denn)
7 Unsere Schule hat einen eigenen Bus. Wir fahren oft zu Sportwettkämpfen. (weil)
8 Die Eltern sind immer sehr gut informiert. Die Schule hat eine Webseite mit aktuellen Nachrichten. (denn)
9 Jüngere Schüler lernen Schwimmen im Sportunterricht. Unsere Schule hat einen kleinen Pool. (weil)
10 Ich gehe gern zur Schule. Ich habe meine Freunde dort. (denn)

### Remember

Remember what happens to the word order after **weil** ('the verb runs a mile'), in contrast to **denn**, which does not change the word order. However, both require a comma to precede them.

## Activity 3

 Schulregeln

Complete the sentences with the correct form of the verb in brackets.

1 Man _____ in der Schule nicht rauchen. (dürfen)
2 Man _____ pünktlich zum Unterricht kommen. (müssen)
3 Ich _____ mein Handy mit zur Schule bringen. (können)
4 Aber ich _____ mein Handy im Unterricht nicht benutzen. (dürfen)
5 Wir _____ die Hausaufgaben in der Schulbibliothek machen. (können)
6 In meiner Schule _____ wir Schuluniform tragen. (müssen)
7 Wir _____ im Unterricht zur Toilette gehen – aber wir _____ den Lehrer fragen. (dürfen, müssen)
8 _____ du in der Schule Kaugummi kauen? (dürfen)
9 Wann _____ du morgens in der Schule sein? (müssen)
10 Wo _____ du Mittag essen? (können)

## Activity 4

 Wie sind deine Lehrer?

Complete the sentences by going one better each time.

**Example:** Frau Schmidt ist lustig, aber Frau Witzig ist lustiger.

1 Herr Klein ist langweilig, aber Herr Schnarchmann ist _____.
2 Frau Winter ist freundlich, aber Frau Sonnenschein ist _____.
3 Herr Hoffmann ist cool, aber Herr Ferrari ist _____.
4 Frau Meisel ist launisch, aber Frau Sauer ist _____.
5 Herr Kern ist motiviert, aber Herr Aktionsmann ist _____.
6 Frau Groß ist hilfsbereit, aber Frau Samariter ist _____.
7 Herr Berg ist musikalisch, aber Herr Singer ist _____.
8 Frau Maus ist kreativ, aber Frau Künstler ist _____.
9 Herr Schmidt ist sportlich, aber Herr Renner ist _____.
10 Frau Siemens ist geduldig, aber Frau Zeitner ist _____.

## Activity 5

 Wortstellung

Put the words in the right order to make meaningful sentences in the future tense.

1 mit 16 – werde – die Schule – verlassen – Ich
2 wird – Meine Schwester – studieren – Medizin – in Edinburgh
3 du – wirst – das Abitur – machen – Wann

*Remember*

Whenever there are two verbs in a German sentence, the second one has to go to the end.

4  ich – Später – werde – wohnen – in einer Großstadt
5  Vielleicht – ich – in Deutschland – machen – ein Brückenjahr – werde
6  werden – eine Weltreise – machen – Mein Freund und ich
7  wird – Mein Vater – im September – bekommen – einen neuen Job
8  Meine Eltern und ich – fliegen – werden – nach Berlin – im Sommer
9  werde – Mit 18 Jahren – ich – meine Fahrerlaubnis – machen
10  In der Zukunft – heiraten – ich – werde

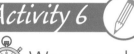 **Activity 6**

 Wann machen wir das?

Match the time phrases.

| | | | |
|---|---|---|---|
| 1 | am Wochenende | a) | at midday |
| 2 | jeden Tag | b) | on Friday |
| 3 | mittwochs | c) | in the afternoon |
| 4 | am Freitag | d) | at the weekend |
| 5 | um 9 Uhr | e) | early in the morning(s) |
| 6 | um 16 Uhr | f) | every day |
| 7 | früh morgens | g) | at 9 a.m. |
| 8 | in der Mittagszeit | h) | next year |
| 9 | nächstes Jahr | i) | at 4 p.m. |
| 10 | am Nachmittag | j) | Wednesdays |

## Check this out!

### Prepositions

Prepositions are very small words which have a huge effect on the German adjectives and nouns following them. You will have come across *mit* and *in*, which are followed by the dative case. In the dative case, the articles *der, die, das* change as follows:

der Bus – mit/in dem Bus (by/in the bus)
ein Bus – mit/in einem Bus
das Auto – mit/in dem Auto (by/in the car)
ein Auto – mit/in einem Auto
die Klasse – mit/in der Klasse (with/in the class)
eine Klasse – mit/in einer Klasse

**Remember**

For masculine (*der*) and neuter (*das*) nouns, *in dem* is fused to *im*.

73

## Activity 7

### Der Dativ

Complete the following sentences by changing the article of the noun in brackets to the dative case. Be careful, as the preposition may also change.

1 Ich fahre mit _____ (das) Fahrrad zur Schule.
2 Ich habe meine Schultasche in _____ (das) Auto vergessen.
3 Thomas sitzt in _____ (die) Klasse neben mir.
4 Die Hausaufgaben stehen in _____ (das) Hausaufgabenheft.
5 Meine Klasse kommt gut mit _____ (der) Englischlehrer aus.
6 Ich komme nicht gut mit _____ (die) Chemielehrerin aus.
7 Gestern bin ich in _____ (die) Sportstunde gefallen – aber ich bin okay.
8 Manchmal habe ich Probleme mit _____ (das) Schulessen, denn es schmeckt nicht so gut.
9 Viele Schüler kaufen das Mittagessen in _____ (ein) Café oder in _____ (der) Supermarkt.
10 Meine Schule ist in _____ (die) Stadtmitte, sodass viele Schüler mit _____ (die) Straßenbahn oder mit _____ (der) Zug zur Schule kommen.

## Activity 8

### Mein Alltag

Translate the following sentences into German. Remember to use the correct verb endings and word order.

1 School starts (begins) at 9 a.m.
2 I go to school by bus every day.
3 On Wednesdays there is a sports club in school.
4 On Friday I have double Maths – that's great!
5 At midday we have lunch (we eat) in the school canteen.
6 I come home at 4 p.m.
7 Next year I will stay on at school.
8 At the weekend I do my homework and visit my friends.
9 I study (learn) for tests early in the morning.
10 I watch TV in the afternoon.

## Activity 9

 Wie findest du Schuluniform?

Express your opinion about school uniforms in German. Use the phrases *Meiner Meinung nach* and *Ich bin der Meinung, dass …*

**Example:** Schuluniform ist praktisch.
  a) Meiner Meinung nach ist Schuluniform praktisch.
  b) Ich bin der Meinung, dass Schuluniform praktisch ist.
1 Schuluniform ist altmodisch und lästig.
2 Man verliert durch Schuluniform seine Individualität.
3 Man hat mit Schuluniform ein Team-Gefühl.
4 Man ist bei Klassenfahrten durch Schuluniform sicherer.
5 Schuluniform kann manchmal teuer sein.
6 Alle Schüler sehen mit Schuluniform gleich aus.
7 Schuluniform verhindert Mobbing in der Schule.
8 Markenkleidung sollte man nicht in der Schule tragen.
9 Man kann in der Freizeit Markenkleidung tragen.
10 Schuluniform löst das Mobbing-Problem nicht.

> **Remember**
>
> The verb is always the second idea in a German sentence – unless there is a subordinating conjunction (connector) which sends the verb to the end.

> to look alike
> (separable verb)
> *aussehen*

## Activity 10

 Meine Schule

**Read the passage about a school. Find the German equivalent for the English words and phrases on the next page.**

Seit vier Jahren besuche ich die Friedrich-Schiller-Gesamtschule in Weimar. Das ist eine relativ große und ziemlich bekannte Stadt im Südosten von Deutschland.

Meine Schule hat etwa 500 Schülerinnen und Schüler und ungefähr 40 Lehrerinnen und Lehrer. Der Schultag beginnt um acht Uhr und endet um 14 Uhr. Nach der Schule gibt es viele Klubs und Aktivitäten, weil meine Schule eine Ganztagsschule ist.

Jeden Tag habe ich sechs Stunden, eine kleine und eine große Pause sowie eine Mittagspause, damit man in der Schulkantine essen kann. Jede Stunde dauert 45 Minuten – das finde ich gut. In der großen Pause treffe ich meine Freunde auf dem Schulhof und wir quatschen über das Fernsehprogramm oder über die neusten Schulgeschichten.

Mein Lieblingsfach ist Geschichte, weil ich das echt interessant und super spannend finde. Die Lehrerin kann toll erklären, wir sehen oft DVDs oder Clips

aus dem Internet. Aber mein Horrorfach ist Sport, denn ich bin total unsportlich. Ich interessiere mich auch nicht für Werken oder Hauswirtschaft. Manchmal denke ich, dass ich zwei linke Hände habe. Ich bin sehr gut in Englisch und Französisch aber nicht so gut in Chemie und Physik.

In unserer Schule gibt es keine Schuluniform, aber wir haben andere Schultraditionen: Jede Klasse macht eine Klassenfahrt pro Jahr, wir haben fünf Exkursionstage von September bis Juni und die Lehrer organisieren eine Weihnachtsdisko und eine Disko zum Valentinstag.

Ich finde meine Schule toll, weil wir wie eine große Familie sind. Die meisten Lehrer sind motiviert und arbeiten gern mit uns. Später würde ich sehr gern Fremdsprachen an der Universität studieren und auch ein Jahr im Ausland leben.

1 comprehensive school
2 the school day starts
3 all-day-school
4 a lunch break
5 in the playground
6 the latest school stories
7 The teacher can explain (things) very well.
8 I am also not interested in
9 two left hands
10 I am very good at
11 one school trip per year
12 like a big family
13 most teachers
14 foreign languages
15 abroad

# Employability

  Arbeit

Match the job description to the correct job below.

1 Ich repariere Autos und Motorräder.
2 Ich arbeite in einem Krankenhaus und habe oft Nachtschicht.
3 Ich unterrichte kleine Kinder im Lesen und Schreiben sowie Mathematik.
4 Jeden Morgen bringe ich Briefe und kleine Päckchen zu den Leuten.
5 Ich arbeite in einem Büro und schreibe E-mails, kopiere Dokumente und telefoniere sehr viel.
6 Ich plane und zeichne Häuser, Brücken und andere Gebäude.
7 Ich arbeite für Klienten und helfe ihnen bei rechtlichen Problemen.
8 Ich helfe Kindern, die in der Schule Probleme haben.
9 Jeden Tag fliege ich eine Passagiermaschine durch Europa.
10 Ich baue Fenster und Türen ein und kann auch Möbel fertigen.

a) der Architekt/die Architektin
b) der Grundschullehrer/die Grundschullehrerin
c) der Pilot/die Pilotin
d) der Mechaniker/die Mechanikerin
e) der Tischler/die Tischlerin
f) der Krankenpfleger/die Krankenschwester
g) der Sekretär/die Sekretärin
h) der Postbote/die Postbotin
i) der Integrationshelfer/die Integrationshelferin
j) der Rechtsanwalt/die Rechtsanwältin

## Activity 2

### Freundlich oder unfreundlich?

Choose the correct adjectives to describe what qualities people should have in their jobs.

1  Eine Lehrerin sollte unfreundlich/freundlich und geduldig/ungeduldig sein.
2  Ein Arzt sollte hilfsbereit/unmotiviert und intelligent/dumm sein.
3  Ein Kellner sollte schnell/langsam und höflich/unhöflich sein.
4  Ein Sozialarbeiter sollte ruhig/hektisch und interessiert/desinteressiert sein.
5  Eine Sekretärin sollte neugierig/diskret und ordentlich/unordentlich sein.
6  Ein Taxifahrer sollte launisch/ausgeglichen und humorvoll/humorlos sein.
7  Ein Schulleiter sollte streng/gelassen und fair/unfair sein.
8  Ein Reiseleiter sollte langweilig/unternehmungslustig sein.
9  Eine Verkäuferin sollte aufmerksam/unaufmerksam und schüchtern/selbstbewusst sein.
10  Ein Polizist sollte sportlich/unsportlich und klug/doof sein.

> part-time job
> *der Nebenjob*

## Activity 3

### Nebenjobs

Complete the texts with the missing words.

**Torsten**

Ich habe einen Nebenjob in einem _____ am Stadtrand. Dort _____ ich jeden Samstag von 8 Uhr bis _____. Normalerweise _____ ich Regale auf und helfe im Lager, aber manchmal muss ich auch an der Kasse arbeiten oder saubermachen. Der Job ist gut bezahlt – ich _____ €6 pro _____. Man muss immer freundlich und _____ sein, wenn man mit _____ spricht. Ich arbeite _____ im Supermarkt – aber für immer ist das _____ für mich!

| | | | |
|---|---|---|---|
| *Supermarkt* | *Kunden* | *fülle* | *verdiene* |
| *höflich* | *nichts* | *16 Uhr* | *Stunde* |
| *gern* | *arbeite* | | |

**Marina**

Jedes _____ arbeite ich an einer _____ Tankstelle in der Stadtmitte. Samstags arbeite ich sechs

⇨

Stunden und _____ sind es _____ vier Stunden – zum Glück, denn ich finde den Job _____ langweilig. Ich mache Kaffee und warme _____, verkaufe _____ und helfe in der Waschanlage. Das Gute ist, dass ich ein _____ Geld verdiene und manchmal Trinkgeld bekomme. Ich _____ auf einen modernen _____.

| total | Wochenende | bisschen | Snacks | kleinen | Laptop |
|-------|-----------|----------|--------|---------|--------|
| nur | spare | Zeitungen | sonntags | | |

## Activity 4 ✏

### ⏱ Ein Vorstellungsgespräch

**a)** Match the German and English questions. You are most likely to hear these in a job interview.

1 Erzählen Sie uns etwas über sich.
2 Welches sind Ihre besonderen Stärken und wo sehen Sie Ihre Schwächen?
3 Warum möchten Sie diesen Job?
4 Was sind Ihre Hobbys?
5 Welche Pläne haben Sie für die nächsten fünf Jahre?
6 Was für Gehaltsvorstellungen haben Sie?

a) Why do you want this job?
b) Tell us something about yourself.
c) What are your plans for the next five years?
d) What are your particular strengths and where do you see your weaknesses?
e) What are your hobbies?
f) What are your salary expectations?

**b)** Match these German answers to the questions above. Then translate the answers into English.

(i) In meiner Freizeit spiele ich Tennis und ich gehe schwimmen. Außerdem surfe ich oft im Internet und chatte mit meinen Freunden.

(ii) Ich heiße Anna Tolson und ich bin 18 Jahre alt. Seit meiner Geburt wohne ich in Edinburg. Ich spreche Englisch und seit sechs Jahren lerne ich Deutsch in der Schule.

(iii) In den nächsten fünf Jahren möchte ich gern arbeiten um mehr Erfahrungen zu sammeln. Dann möchte ich gern eine Leitungsstelle übernehmen und mehr Verantwortung tragen.

(iv) Dieser Job interessiert mich sehr, denn ich habe viel über die Firma im Internet gelesen. Ich denke, dass ich die richtige Person für diese Stelle bin.

(v) Ich bin sehr gut in Fremdsprachen und habe ein Talent für Kommunikation. Ich kann sehr gut planen und organisieren. Meine Mathematikkenntnisse könnten ein bisschen besser sein.

(vi) Ich denke, dass ich nicht weniger Geld verdienen möchte als bisher. Die Bezahlung soll der Verantwortung entsprechen.

| job interview | das Vorstellungsgespräch |
|---|---|

# Activity 5

 Das Perfekt

a) Choose the correct auxiliary in the following perfect tense sentences. Remember that verbs of motion (travelling involving a destination) use *sein* (to be) rather than *haben*.

1   Letztes Jahr habe/bin ich ein Arbeitspraktikum in einem Hotel gemacht.
2   Morgens habe/bin ich mit dem Bus zur Arbeit gefahren.
3   Im Hotel habe/bin ich an der Rezeption und in der Küche geholfen.
4   Nach der Arbeit habe/bin ich mit den anderen Kollegen ins Kino oder ins Café gegangen.
5   Die Arbeit hat/ist mir gut gefallen.

b) Choose the correct past participle to complete each sentence so that it makes sense.

1   Im Oktober habe ich eine Woche in einer Gärtnerei gemacht/gearbeitet/gekocht.
2   Dort bin ich morgens mit dem Chef auf den Markt gegegessen/gekauft/gefahren.
3   Dann habe ich im Geschäft geholfen/gesungen/gelesen.
4   Am Nachmittag habe ich das Geschäft sauber gefaulenzt/gemacht/getrunken.
5   Um 17 Uhr bin ich dann nach Hause getanzt/gefallen/gegangen.

c) Remember that the auxiliary changes if the person changes. The past participle will not change. Choose the correct form of auxiliary in each of the following sentences.

1   Im September habe/hat/haben ich in einem kleinen Café in der Stadtmitte gearbeitet.
2   Meine Freundin Tina habe/hat/haben ihr Arbeitspraktikum in einem Sportgeschäft neben dem Café gemacht.
3   Tina und ich bin/ist/sind morgens mit der Straßenbahn in die Stadt gefahren.
4   Wir habe/hat/haben um 9 Uhr mit der Arbeit begonnen.
5   In der Mittagspause bin/ist/sind Tina ins Café gekommen.
6   Dann habe/hat/haben wir Mittag gegessen und geredet.
7   Um 15 Uhr bin/ist/sind wir dann zu Fuß nach Hause gegangen.
8   Wir habe/hat/haben das Arbeitspraktikum gut gefunden.

In your Writing Course Assessment, one of the predictable bullet points is about work experience. This is a good opportunity to show your ability to express the past using the perfect tense.

## Activity 6

### Präpositionen

As previously mentioned, prepositions are little words, but they have a big impact on the noun or pronoun to which they relate. They change the case of the noun or pronoun.

Complete the sentences below with the correct preposition from the list below.

1 Meine Freundin und ich arbeiten _____ einer Woche _____ einem großen Supermarkt.

2 Morgens fahren wir _____ dem Bus – die Bushaltestelle ist direkt _____ meinem Haus.

3 Jeden Tag stellen wir das Obst und Gemüse _____ die Regale und manchmal bringen wir den Müll _____ den Supermarkt, wo die Tonnen stehen.

4 Meine Freundin und ich sparen das Geld _____ einen Urlaub an der Ostsee, denn wir wollen gern _____ die Eltern Ferien machen.

5 Wenn wir abends _____ dem Supermarkt kommen, sind wir oft müde und wollen schnell _____ Hause.

ohne *without*      für *for*      aus *out of*      mit *with/by*      nach *to/after*      hinter *behind*

auf *on/onto*    vor *before/in front of*      seit *since/for (time)*      in *in/into*

## Activity 7

### Was möchtest du später einmal werden?

a) What would you like to be? Give the feminine job titles.

| | |
|---|---|
| 1 der Polizist | 6 der Lehrer |
| 2 der Mechaniker | 7 der Sekretär |
| 3 der Arzt | 8 der Verkäufer |
| 4 der Taxifahrer | 9 der Pilot |
| 5 der Kellner | 10 der Schulleiter |

b) Say in German what the following people want to be. Make sentences.

**Example:** Frank – Tierpfleger im Zoo. (———→) Frank möchte Tierpfleger im Zoo werden.

1 Sabine – Tischlerin in einer Holzwerkstatt

2 Bernd – Kurier bei einem Paketservice

3 Mandy – Sekretärin in einem Autohaus

4 Torsten – Servicekraft bei McDonalds

5 Astrid – Pilotin bei der Lufthansa

6 Martin – Friseur in einem Salon in der Innenstadt

7 Diana – Stuntfrau im Filmstudio

8 Peter – Kranfahrer auf einer großen Baustelle

9 Claudia – Bäuerin mit eigenem Hof

10 Jörg – Krimiautor für einen großen Verlag

## Activity 8

### Pläne

There are a number of ways to talk about plans for the future in German. You can use the following verbs:

*möchten* would like          *wollen* want to          *werden* will

But there is also the verb *vorhaben* (to intend to). It is a separable verb and is followed by a comma and *zu* + infinitive:

*Ich habe vor, nach der Schule in Glasgow zu studieren.*

 Say in German what the following people intend to do. Remember that the verb ending changes when the person changes.

1  Britta – eine Weltreise machen
2  Jens – einen Mercedes fahren
3  Doris und Maren – auf einem Kreuzfahrtschiff arbeiten
4  ich – Pferde züchten
5  Silke – auf den Eiffelturm in Paris steigen
6  Kevin – nach New York fliegen
7  Nicole und Gerd – eine Familie gründen
8  Steffen – Profifußballer werden
9  Markus – in einer Talentshow singen
10 Nancy und Boris – ein neues Computerspiel entwickeln

## Activity 9

### The concept of *Sie* in German

As your German teacher will have pointed out to you, German people use a formal way of addressing each other at work or if they do not know each other well. For this purpose, they use *Sie* (with capital spelling to show that it's a formal pronoun, rather than *sie*, which means 'she' or 'they'). The verb ending changes into plural and the pronoun gets a capital letter.

sie (she) – ihr/ihre (her)
sie (they) – ihr/ihre (their)
Sie (you) – Ihr/Ihre (your)

 Rewrite the following questions in formal German.

1  Wie heißt du?
2  Wo wohnst du?
3  Hast du Geschwister?
4  Wofür interessierst du dich?
5  Was machst du in deiner Freizeit?
6  Welche Fremdsprachen sprichst du?
7  Was sind deine Stärken?
8  Hast du eine Fahrerlaubnis?
9  Kannst du Golf spielen?
10 Möchtest du einen Kaffee mit mir trinken?

## Activity 10

 Studieren oder eine Lehre machen?

Going to university or doing an apprenticeship/job training? Read the following four statements and complete the table below with the correct information in English.

**Anja:** Also, ich möchte auf jeden Fall studieren. Ich interessiere mich für Tiere und deshalb habe ich vor, Tiermedizin zu studieren. Wenn man ein Studium gemacht hat, verdient man auch mehr Geld.

**Tom:** Nee – ein Studium ist nichts für mich, weil ich das langweilig finde. Am liebsten möchte ich aktiv arbeiten und deshalb habe ich vor, eine Lehre als Fleischer in einem Geschäft in der Stadtmitte zu machen. Dann verdiene ich auch

gleich Geld, sodass ich meinen Eltern nicht auf der Tasche liegen muss.

**Svenja:** Studieren? Das dauert mir viel zu lange. Mein Vater hat eine eigene Autowerkstatt. Schon als kleines Mädchen habe ich ihm geholfen Autos und Motorräder zu reparieren. Ich werde in unserem Familienbetrieb eine Lehre als Automechanikerin machen.

**Mark:** Naja, ich möchte Architekt werden und ohne Studium geht das nicht. Aber zuerst werde ich eine Lehre als Baufacharbeiter machen, damit ich praktische Erfahrungen sammeln kann. Danach gehe ich dann zur Uni und mache meinen Magister.

| Name | University or apprenticeship | Reasons for their decision |
|------|------------------------------|----------------------------|
| Anja | | |
| Tom | | |
| Svenja | | |
| Mark | | |

# Culture

## Activity 1

 Was für ein Ferientyp ist das?

Read the following statements. Decide what kind of holiday each person likes. Underline words and phrases that support your answer.

**Sabine:** Meine Familie und ich fahren sehr gern im Winter in die Berge. Dort wohnen wir in einem Chalet und laufen Ski, gehen Snowboard fahren oder Schlittschuh laufen. Der Schnee und die Kälte stören uns nicht – ich liebe Winterferien!

> type of holiday
> *der Ferientyp*

⇨

**Ralph:** Meine Eltern und ich fahren am liebsten in den Süden. Jedes Jahr fliegen wir auf eine Insel im Mittelmeer, wo wir in einer Villa direkt am Strand wohnen. Die Sonne scheint, es ist super warm und ich kann jeden Tag im Meer baden oder im Pool schwimmen. Herrlich!

**Andreas:** Ich fahre sehr gern zelten. Jedes Jahr fährt meine Familie mit dem Wohnmobil und einem kleinen Zelt für mich und meinen Bruder an die Ostsee. Wir sind sehr gern in der Natur – und auf dem Campingplatz ist immer etwas los. Dort sind viele andere Jugendliche, sodass wir schnell Freunde finden.

**Vanessa:** Also ich fahre am liebsten übers Wochenende in eine europäische Großstadt, um die Sehenswürdigkeiten zu besuchen und eine andere Kultur und Sprache kennen zu lernen. Im letzten Jahr war ich in London und Madrid, dieses Jahr steht Hamburg auf dem Programm und von dort aus fliege ich dann nach Edinburg. Ich liebe Geschichte, Museen und Ausstellungen. Kultur ist mir sehr wichtig.

## Activity 2

 Berlin – die Hauptstadt von Deutschland

a) Join the sentence beginnings with the correct endings, so that it makes sense in German.

| | |
|---|---|
| 1 Berlin ist mit 3,4 Millionen Einwohnern die größte Stadt Deutschlands | a) weil es in der Stadtmitte viele Parks gibt. |
| 2 Berlin ist auch eine sehr wasserreiche Stadt, | b) und sogar neunmal größer als Paris! |
| 3 Viele Touristen sagen, dass Berlin sehr grün ist, | c) sind typische Spezialitäten aus Berlin. |
| 4 Die Stadt ist bekannt für ihre Sehenswürdigkeiten, zum Beispiel | d) denn sie liegt an den Flüssen Spree und Havel und hat außerdem den Wannsee. |
| 5 Die Currywurst, der Pfannkuchen und die Erbsensuppe | e) für das Brandenburger Tor und den Fernsehturm auf dem Alexanderplatz im Osten der Stadt. |
| 6 Nach dem zweiten Weltkrieg hatte Berlin vier Teile – | f) hat eine Mauer die Stadt Berlin sowie Ost- und Westdeutschland geteilt. |
| 7 Vom 13. August 1961 bis zum 9. November 1989 | g) bei Studenten aus aller Welt. |
| 8 Heute gibt es die Mauer nur noch im Museum, | h) den britischen, den amerikanischen, den französischen und den russischen Sektor. |
| 9 Berlin ist sehr beliebt bei internationalen Touristen und | i) damit man diese Zeit der Trennung nicht vergisst. |
| 10 Man kann die deutsche Hauptstadt in etwa 90 Minuten | j) mit dem Flugzeug von Glasgow oder Manchester erreichen. |

⇒

**b)** Complete the text about Berlin with the words in the box below.

Berlin ist die _____ von Deutschland und befindet sich im _____ des Landes. In Berlin _____ etwa 3,4 _____ Menschen; das _____ der Stadt ist der Berliner _____. Berlin liegt am _____ Spree.

Berlin hat viele _____ Sehenswürdigkeiten. Im _____ der Stadt ist der Alexanderplatz mit der Weltzeituhr und dem _____, der 365 Meter hoch ist. Die breite Straße Unter-den-Linden führt durch das _____ Tor in den Westen der Stadt. In der Nähe ist der _____, das Parlamentsgebäude Deutschlands.

Die größte Einkaufsstraße Berlins heißt _____ – die Berliner sagen auch

„Ku'damm". Dort gibt es viele Geschäfte und das _____ mit Restaurants und Souvenirläden.

Berlin hat einen Zoo im Westen der Stadt und einen _____ im Osten. Es gibt auch viele Theater und _____.

Jedes Jahr kommen viele _____ nach Berlin. Sie besuchen die _____ und Kirchen und machen eine _____ auf der Spree.

| | | |
|---|---|---|
| Tierpark | Touristen | interessante |
| Reichstag | Europacenter | Hauptstadt |
| leben | Osten (×2) | Bär |
| Brandenburger | Museen | Millionen |
| Fluss | Kurfürstendamm | Symbol |
| Fernsehturm | Kabaretts | Bootsfahrt |

 **Activity 3**

 Der Schwarzwald – Eine Urlaubsregion in Baden Württemberg

Read the following text about the Black Forest. Answer the questions in German. Make sentences.

Baden Württemberg ist ein Bundesland im Süden von Deutschland. Dort leben etwa 10,7 Millionen Menschen und es ist das drittgrößte Bundesland Deutschlands.

Die Hauptstadt von Baden Württemberg heißt Stuttgart und hat etwa 500.000 Einwohner.

Stuttgart ist bekannt für seine Autoproduktion. Dort ist der Hauptsitz von Mercedes Benz. Außerdem gibt es in Stuttgart einen sehr erfolgreichen Fußballverein – den VfB Stuttgart.

Der Schwarzwald ist eine Region in Baden Württemberg. Dort gibt es Wälder, Seen und Berge. Jedes Jahr kommen sehr viele Touristen aus dem In– und Ausland in den Schwarzwald.

⇒

 **Remember**

You can always 'steal' vocabulary from the question to make your answer.

Ein beliebtes Souvenir ist die Kuckucksuhr. Es gibt auch typische Spezialitäten aus dem Schwarzwald wie die Schwarzwälder Kirschtorte und den Schwarzwälder Schinken. Sie sind in der ganzen Welt bekannt.

1 Wo liegt Baden Württemberg?
2 Wie viele Menschen wohnen dort?
3 Wie heißt die Hauptstadt des Bundeslandes?
4 Wofür ist Stuttgart bekannt?
5 Was gibt es im Schwarzwald?
6 Was ist die Kuckucksuhr?
7 Welche typischen Spezialitäten gibt es im Schwarzwald?

## Activity 4

 Glasgow und Edinburgh – zwei schottische Großstädte

a) Read the statements below and decide whether they describe Glasgow or Edinburgh.

1 Diese Stadt ist seit 1437 schottische Hauptstadt.
2 In dieser Stadt leben etwa 400.000 Einwohner.
3 In dieser Stadt leben etwa 600.000 Einwohner.
4 Diese schottische Stadt hat vier Universitäten.
5 Die traditionelle Wirtschaft dieser Stadt ist „Bücher, Bier und Kekse."
6 Diese Stadt ist als Arbeiterstadt bekannt.
7 Der Höhepunkt der kulturellen Lebens in dieser Stadt ist das sommerliche Festival.
8 In dieser Stadt findet der zweitgrößte Marathon des Vereinten Königreichs statt.
9 Amerikanischer Tabak wurde in diese Stadt importiert.
10 Diese Stadt ist die zweitbeste Einkaufsstadt im Vereinigten Königreich.

b) Rewrite the following sentences. Start with the conditional clause.

**Example:**
Man kann einkaufen gehen, wenn es regnet.
Wenn es regnet, kann man einkaufen gehen.

1 Man kann mit der U-Bahn fahren, wenn es regnet.
2 Man kann zum Straßenmarkt Barras gehen, wenn es regnet.
3 Man kann Galerien und Museen besuchen, wenn es regnet.
4 Man kann in einem Restaurant oder in einer Kneipe essen gehen, wenn es regnet.
5 Man kann das nationale Fußballmuseum im Hampden Park besuchen, wenn es regnet.

> ### Remember
>
> *Was kann man in Glasgow machen, wenn es regnet?* Remember there is an inversion after the comma — the conditional part using *wenn* will become the 'first idea'. The verb will always insist on being 'the second idea' in a German sentence.

⇨

   6  Man kann mit dem Zug nach Edinburgh fahren, wenn es regnet.

   7  Man kann ins St Enoch Zentrum gehen, wenn es regnet.

   8  Man kann einen Bummel in der Buchanan Street machen, wenn es regnet.

   9  Man kann im Bett bleiben, wenn es regnet.

## Activity 5

 Das Perfekt und das Futur

Turn the following present tense sentences into perfect tense and future tense sentences.

**Example:** Ich **fliege** mit Lufthansa nach Deutschland. (present tense)

   **a)** Ich **bin** mit Lufthansa nach Deutschland **geflogen**. (perfect tense)

   **b)** Ich **werde** mit Lufthansa nach Deutschland **fliegen**. (future tense)

1  Meine Eltern und ich **wohnen** in einem Hotel in der Stadtmitte von Hamburg.

2  Mein Vater **macht** eine Hafenrundfahrt mit einem kleinen Schiff.

3  Meine Mutter und ich **besuchen** das Miniaturmuseum in der Speicherstadt.

4  An einem Abend **sehen** wir das Musical „Tarzan".

5  Ich **kaufe** für meine Freunde T-Shirts in Hamburg.

## Activity 6

 Wenn

Join the sentences using *wenn*. Remember the position of the verb in the main clause and in the *wenn* clause. There are two ways of joining them – attempt both.

1  Ich habe genug Geld gespart. Ich fahre nach London.

2  Meine Eltern haben Urlaub. Sie fliegen nach Amerika.

3  Meine Klasse fährt nach Berlin. Wir machen eine Stadtrundfahrt.

4  Mein Austauschpartner kommt nach Schottland. Ich fahre mit ihm zum Loch Ness.

5  Ich besuche Deutschland. Ich möchte München und die Alpen sehen.

## Activity 7

### Welches Wort?

Complete the questions with the correct question word in the list below. Look at the answer for help.

1  _____ warst du in den Ferien? Meine Familie und ich waren in München.

2  _____ warst du dort? Wir waren zehn Tage dort.

3  _____ hast du in München gewohnt? Meine Eltern haben eine Ferienwohnung gemietet.

4  _____ habt ihr in den zehn Tagen gemacht? Wir haben München gesehen und sind auch in die Alpen gefahren.

5  _____ bist du nach München gefahren? Wir sind mit dem Flugzeug von Edinburg geflogen.

6  _____ hat euch zum Flughafen in Edinburg gebracht? Wir sind selbst gefahren und haben das Auto im Parkhaus abgestellt.

7  _____ seid ihr nach München gefahren? Mein Vater wird nächstes Jahr für eine britische Firma in München arbeiten und wir wollten die Stadt kennen lernen.

**When?** *Wann?*　**Who?** *Wer?*　**How?** *Wie?*　**What?** *Was?*
**Where?** *Wo?*　**How long?** *Wie lange?*　**Why?** *Warum?*

### Remember

Remember to use the correct word order:
Time – Manner – Place.

## Activity 8

### Wortstellung

Translate these sentences into German, using the correct time phrase.

1  We are going to Dresden in two weeks.

2  This week I am booking the flights on the internet.

3  At the weekend my friend is going to buy a book about Dresden in the bookshop.

4  My parents are going to change Euros in the bank tomorrow.

5  My grandmother is baking biscuits for the journey next week.

### Hints & tips

*Although these sentences refer to the future, simply use the verbs in the present tense as that is what most Germans do.*

## Activity 9

### Deutsche Feiertage

Read the following passage and find the German words and phrases for the English below.

Die Deutschen feiern gern und oft – aber welche Feiertage sind eigentlich besonders wichtig für deutsche Familien?

An erster Stelle steht das Weihnachtsfest als Fest der Familie am Jahresende. Am 24. Dezember ist Heiligabend und die Kinder bekommen ihre Geschenke. Am 25. Dezember gibt es ein großes Weihnachtsessen – manche Familien essen Gans, andere essen Truthahn oder sogar Fisch. Die Geschäfte sind am 25. Dezember und am 26. Dezember geschlossen, sodass niemand zur Arbeit gehen muss.

Das zweitwichtigste Familienfest ist das Osterfest im Frühling. Die Kinder bemalen Eier und dekorieren damit den Osterstrauß. Am Ostersonntag gehen viele Leute in die Kirche, bevor sie mit der Familie Mittag essen. Der Osterhase bringt den Kindern Schokoladeneier – aber man muss sie im Garten oder im Haus suchen.

Und dann gibt es auch neue Traditionen, die aus anderen Ländern nach Deutschland gekommen sind. Am 14. Februar feiert man in Deutschland den Valentinstag und am 31. Oktober gibt es auch deutsche Kinder, die von Haus zu Haus gehen und „Süßes oder Saures" rufen. Halloween steht nach Weihnachten und Ostern an dritter Stelle beim Verkauf von Schokolade und Süßigkeiten.

Das Internet und Kinofilme haben dafür gesorgt, dass britische und amerikanische Traditionen nach Deutschland gekommen sind – ein Resultat der Globalisierung im 21. Jahrhundert.

1  especially important
2  family festivity at the end of the year
3  a big Christmas dinner
4  The shops are closed.
5  in spring
6  on Easter Sunday
7  the Easter bunny
8  new traditions
9  trick or treat
10  in third place
11  movies
12  a result of globalisation

# Activity 10

## Feiertag!

Match the dates with the correct German festival or public holiday.

| | | | |
|---|---|---|---|
| 1 | Silvester | a) | 3. Oktober |
| 2 | Tag der deutschen Einheit | b) | 1. Januar |
| 3 | Reformationstag | c) | 31. Oktober |
| 4 | Muttertag | d) | 31. Dezember |
| 5 | Internationaler Frauentag | e) | 1. September |
| 6 | Kindertag | f) | 8. März |
| 7 | Weltfriedenstag | g) | 1. Juni |
| 8 | Neujahr | h) | 1. November |
| 9 | Vatertag/Christi Himmelfahrt | i) | 11. November |
| 10 | Nikolaustag | j) | 6. Dezember |
| 11 | Allerseelen | k) | am zweiten Sonntag im Mai |
| 12 | Martinstag | l) | am vierzigsten Tag nach Ostern |

# Vocabulary

Before you get ready for an assessment, especially in listening and reading, check that you know the vocabulary you need to succeed. In the course of your German lessons, get into the habit of noting down words and phrases you find helpful. Try to use these in a sentence rather than on their own.

## Check this out!

There are different strategies for learning vocabulary:

★ categorise words according to word families or use headwords
★ use sticky pads to note down words and phrases and stick them up in your room
★ draw pictures and label them with the words you need to learn
★ learn them as opposites
★ talk to yourself in German or read phrases and sentences out loud.

It all depends on your learning style. Try and see what works best for you.

To pass National 5 German, you should cover the following areas:

## General vocabulary

- Numbers (times, including 24 hour clock, dates, distances and prices)
- Days of the week, months, weeks and years
- Colours and clothes
- Weather
- Food and drink
- Countries and nationalities

## Society

- Family (members of the family, describing character and appearance, describing relationships within the family, different types of family)
- Friends (reasons for friendship, relationship problems)
- Lifestyles (eating and drinking habits, teenage problems)
- Media (music, TV habits, modern media in the life of teenagers)
- Language learning (opinion about languages and language learning, languages in a work environment, languages in a European context)
- Places in a town and neighbourhood (describe home town/ neighbourhood, life in a town and in the country)

## Learning

- School subjects and your opinion on them
- Your school (school day, school uniform, school traditions)
- Teachers and what you think of them

- Your strengths and weaknesses
- School in Germany and school in Scotland

## Employability

- Jobs and job descriptions
- Personality traits for specific jobs
- Future career plans
- Details and opinions about work experience

## Culture

- Different types of holidays
- Planning a trip
- A holiday in the past/a holiday in the future
- Special events in the German calendar

# Grammar

First of all, grammar is not a dirty word. There is more to it than just structure – it is like a formula that can be studied and applied, once you understand the rules.

Without grammatical knowledge you will struggle to create your own sentences and express yourself in a foreign language.

The biggest issue for English native speakers is German word order (sentence structure). Here are four simple rules which tell you all about it. Learn them and you will be able to make your German sentences with confidence.

## 1  German sentence structure

Well, it is all about the verb(s) really. So let's see if we can approach this systematically …

### 1.1  Simple sentences with one verb

*Meine Freundin Mandy **spielt** seit drei Jahren Gitarre.*
*Meine Freundin Mandy **spielt** seit drei Jahren in der Schülerband Gitarre.*
*Meine Freundin Mandy **spielt** seit drei Jahren mit Begeisterung in der Schülerband Gitarre.*
*Seit drei Jahren **spielt** meine Freundin Mandy mit Begeisterung in der Schülerband Gitarre.*

**Remember**

The verb is always the second idea (not the second word) in a German sentence.

### 1.2  Simple sentences with two verbs

*Meine Freundin Mandy **kann** sehr gut Gitarre **spielen**.*
*Sie **hat** drei Jahre lang in der Schulband Gitarre **gespielt**.*
*Im nächsten Jahr **wird** sie in einer Vorgruppe auf einem Rockkonzert **spielen**.*

**Remember**

Co-ordinating connectors have no impact on the sentence structure.

---

*Hints & tips*

As soon as you have two verbs in a German sentence, one of them has to go to the end. The other remains the second idea of the sentence and is ruled by the subject (the person who carries out the action).

---

### 1.3  Complex sentences with a co-ordinating connector

*Meine Freundin Mandy **spielt** seit drei Jahren Gitarre, denn sie **möchte** Musik **studieren**.*
*Sie **übt** jeden Tag in der Garage und sie **hat** jedes Wochenende ein Konzert mit ihrer Band.*
*Mandy **kann** sehr gut Musik **machen**, aber sie **kann** nicht so gut **kochen**.*

**Remember**

Signal words for co-ordinating connectors:
**denn   aber   und**

## 1.4 Complex sentences with a subordinating connector

*Meine Freundin Mandy **spielt** seit drei Jahren Gitarre. Sie **möchte** Musik **studieren**.*

*Meine Freundin Mandy **spielt** seit drei Jahren Gitarre, weil sie Musik **studieren möchte**.*

*Sie **übt** jeden Tag etwa zwei Stunden. Sie **hat** viele Hausaufgaben.*

*Sie **übt** jeden Tag etwa zwei Stunden, obwohl sie viele Hausaufgaben **hat**.*

*Mandy **plant** ihre Zeit sehr gründlich. Sie **kann** Hobby und Schule unter einen Hut **bringen**.*

*Mandy **plant** ihre Zeit sehr gründlich, sodass sie Hobby und Schule unter einen Hut **bringen kann**.*

**Remember**

Some of the signal words for subordinating connectors: **weil  obwohl  dass sodass  wenn**

## 1.5 Complex sentences with the subordinating part at the front

*Meine Freundin Mandy **spielt** seit drei Jahren Gitarre, **weil** sie Musik studieren **möchte**.*

***Weil** sie Musik studieren **möchte, spielt** meine Freundin Mandy seit drei Jahren Gitarre.*

*Sie **übt** jeden Tag etwa zwei Stunden, **obwohl** sie viele Hausaufgaben **hat**.*

***Obwohl** sie viele Hausaufgaben **hat, übt** sie jeden Tag etwa zwei Stunden.*

*Mandy **plant** ihre Zeit sehr gründlich, **damit** sie Hobby und Schule unter einen Hut bringen **kann**.*

***Damit** sie Hobby und Schule unter einen Hut bringen **kann, plant** Mandy ihre Zeit sehr gründlich.*

**Remember**

Subordinating connectors kick the verb from its second idea position to the end of the sentence.

# 2 Tense forms

As a National 5 student, you should be able to understand and use three tense forms: the present tense, the perfect tense expressing the past, and the future tense. However, as most Germans use the present tense to express the future, life is a bit easier for you than for learners of other languages.

## 2.1 The present tense

You use the present tense in German to make a statement, and to describe things which happen regularly or are happening just now. It is important to learn the verb endings in the present tense as well as irregular forms and modal verbs (*müssen, können, wollen, dürfen, sollen*).

Here are some examples of the present tense:

*Jeden Tag **fahre** ich mit dem Bus zur Schule.*

*Meine beste Freundin **heißt** Sibylle und **ist** 15 Jahre alt.*

*Meine Eltern und ich **besuchen** am Wochenende meine Oma.*

***Kannst** du mir bei den Hausaufgaben **helfen**?*

*Ich **chatte** im Moment mit meinen Freunden.*

**Remember**

The subordinating part at the front keeps its structure with the verb at the end. But after the comma, the main part of the complex sentence is introduced by the verb followed by the subject. This is also known as inversion.

## 2.2 The perfect tense expressing the past

The perfect tense is mostly used in spoken German to talk about past events. It has two parts: a form of *haben* or *sein* (called the auxiliary verb) and the past participle which is always at the end of the sentence.

Here are some examples of the perfect tense:

> *Gestern **bin** ich mit dem Rad zum Supermarkt **gefahren**.*
> *Mein Freund **hat** mir zum Geburtstag ein tolles Parfüm **geschenkt**.*
> *Vor zwei Wochen **haben** meine Eltern ein neues Auto **gekauft**.*
> *Letztes Jahr **sind** wir mit dem Wohnmobil durch Norddeutschland*
>   ***gefahren**.*
> *Ich **habe** im Flugzeug **gelesen** und Musik **gehört**.*

## 2.3 The future tense

You use the future tense to speak about future events. The future tense consists of a form of *werden* (called the auxiliary verb) and the infinitive of the main verb which is always at the end of the sentence. However, most Germans would use the present tense and add a future time phrase, such as *nächste Woche*.

Here are some examples of the future tense:

> *Morgen **werden** wir eine Mathearbeit **schreiben**.*
> *Nächste Woche **wird** meine Cousine zu Besuch **kommen**.*
> *In einem Jahr **werde** ich an der Universität in Berlin **studieren**.*
> *Bald **werden** meine Eltern einen neue Wohnung **haben**.*
> *In zwei Tagen **wird** meine Klasse nach Köln **fahren**.*

# 3 The cases

The concept of case also exists in the English language. However, in German cases play a much bigger role and affect articles, nouns, pronouns and adjectives. They change their form/endings to show which case they are in.

Here are some examples of cases in English:

- **Whose** car is this? This is **my mother's** car. (Genitive – shows possession)
- Can you see Tom? Yes, I can see **him**. (Accusative – direct object to the verb)

In German, there are four cases: **nominative**, **accusative**, **genitive** and **dative**. They all play a specific role and this is what they do in a sentence:

## 3.1 Nominative

The subject of the sentence is in the nominative. This is the person or the thing that carries out the action.

> *Seit einer Woche lernt **mein Bruder** für die Klassenarbeit in Englisch.*
> ***Der Hund** hat gerade meine Hausaufgaben gefressen.*
> ***Meine Mutter** kauft morgen ein Netbook.*
> ***Das neue Haus** hat einen großen Garten.*

## 3.2 Accusative

This case is used for the direct object in a sentence. The direct object is a person or a thing that is directly affected by the verb.

> *Meine Schwester hat letzte Woche **ein interessantes** Buch gelesen.*
> *Ich sehe **deinen Vati** in eurem Auto vor der Schule.*
> *Der Mathelehrer erklärt **eine schwierige Aufgabe**.*
> *Morgen kaufen wir **neue Schuhe** für meinen Bruder.*

## 3.3 Genitive

The genitive case shows possession and is often translated into English using 'of' as well as the use of 's' plus an apostrophe e.g. my sister**'s** book.

> *Der Titel **des neuen Krimis** heißt „Verlorene Tochter".*
> *Das Motorrad **meiner Schwester** muss in die Werkstatt.*
> *Der Sattel **des Pferdes** sitzt zu locker.*
> *Das Zimmer **meiner Geschwister** ist selten aufgeräumt.*

## 3.4 Dative

The dative case is used for the indirect object that is affected by the verb. It is often translated into English using 'to' or 'for'.

> *Meine Mutter hat **meinem Bruder** ein Eis gekauft.*
> *Ich habe **meiner Schwester** bei den Hausaufgaben geholfen.*
> *Der Polizist hilft **dem Kind** über die Straße.*
> *Der Lehrer erklärt **den Eltern** die Klassensituation.*

Please note that a preposition insists that the dative or accusative follow, for example:

> *Ich komme gut **mit meiner** Mutter aus. (dative)*
> *Meine Freunde und ich gehen jeden Tag **in den Park**. (accusative)*
> *Meine Freunde und ich spielen jeden Tag Fußball **in dem/im Park**.*
>    *(dative)*
> *Ralph hat **seit einem Jahr** einen neuen Job. (dative)*

German cases will play a much bigger role in your Higher German class where you will get lots of practice, helping you to understand the logic behind them. For now, the very best of luck for your National 5 German exam!

> *Viel Glück und alles Gute!*

## Chapter 4

### Answers

#### Society

1 Her mother tells her to wash every night. – Her mother tells her to brush her teeth every night. – Her parents want Vanessa to be home at 8 p.m. – Her father phones her (all the time) on her mobile. **(Any three)**

2 Her parents are always there for her. – Her parents have never let Vanessa down. – Her parents help her when she has a problem. **(Any one)**

3 His father works a lot. – His father is often away on business/travelling. – His father is the chairperson of the tennis club. **(Any two)**

4 His father is often stressed. – He is often in a bad mood. – He does not get enough sleep. – He goes to bed after midnight and leaves the house at 7 a.m. **(Any three)**

5 Vanessa and Raphael get on with their parents despite problems.

### Answers

#### Learning

1 **Students:** They are from other nations/countries/states. – They want to work in Germany. – They are older than 18. – They have registered for a German course at the job centre. – They already live in Germany.
**Course:** A course is six months. – There are five periods every day. – Students expand their knowledge of the German language, culture, history and politics. – There is an exam at the end. – Participants receive a certificate.

**Opinion:** It is not so easy at times/with up to 16 nationalities in class. – It is a great feeling when students pass their exam.
**Job prospects:** In 2012 almost one million people from other European countries moved to Germany. – Every year (at least) half a million immigrants come to Germany. – There is lots to do for Susanne in the future.

2 Learning German is important for successful integration.

### Answers

#### Employability

1 Christoph has been working in the leisure pool for nine years. – His hometown is Hannover. – He trained (there) to be a pool assistant. – He completed Realschule/secondary school. **(Any two)**

2 Christoph pays attention/makes sure that nothing happens (in the water). – He checks the water temperature (every morning). – He cleans the filters. – He collects rubbish. – He cleans the toilets. – He (even) sells ice-cream. **(Any three)** ⇨

3 He would like to study sport. – He would like to be a swimming instructor. – He would like to train young swim talents (in a club). – He would like to take part in the Iron-Man-Competition in Hawaii. **(Any two)**

4 Christoph went on a summer holiday. – He went to the Baltic Sea coast last summer. – An elderly gentleman over-estimated his strength. – An elderly gentleman had problems to swim back to shore. – Christoph spotted/saw this. – He was able to help/save him. **(Any three)**

5 Christoph loves his job but wants to better himself.

## Answers

### Culture

1 a) Stephan
   b) Mandy
   c) Thomas
   d) Susanne

2 **Susanne:** The stories were realistic. – It was all about the problems of normal teenagers. – She liked the family/familiar/informal atmosphere. **(Any two)**
   **Mandy:** She finds the main (female) character cool. – She shows that you can change from a shy (and even clumsy) to an attractive person. – She thinks that many young girls are able to identify with the role/the main character. **(Any two)**
   **Thomas:** Young people are at the centre of the soap. – The soap shows the ups and downs of life. – The stories are authentic. **(Any two)**
   **Stephan:** It is the first soap opera for people his age. – The stories are exciting. – The soap opera is gripping. **(Any two)**

3 Soap operas help them to learn more about themselves and their teenage problems.

# Chapter 5

## Answers

### Society monologue

1 a) Christine lives in the same street. – They go to the same school. – They go to the same class. – They meet every morning. – They go to school by bike (together). **(Any two)**
   b) Christine is always **friendly** and **helpful** but she is never **moody**.

2 Thomas (often) bullies Christine. – Thomas (often) annoys Christine. – He calls her small and ugly. – He wrote on her Facebook page (small and ugly). **(Any two)**

3 She listened. – She took notes. – She spoke with Thomas. – She told him to apologise (to Christine). – She did a bullying project with the class. **(Any two)**

4 Bullying needs to be discussed in today's schools.

## Answers

### Learning monologue

1 It is a grammar school. – He is in tenth grade. – He has exams this year. – It is hectic and stressful. – He has lots of homework. – He has lots of tests. **(Any three)**

2 It is not a problem for him. – He is very good in Maths. – He can think logically. – He understands mathematical problems quickly. – He wants to study Maths at university. – It is fun. **(Any two)**

3 He should organise his work (better). – He should spend more time doing homework. – He should learn more (before a test). **(Any two)**

4 He helps his mum in the household (every day). – He helps his mum with his little brother. – He likes to go to the cinema/to the disco with his friends. – His friends are important for him. **(Any three)**

5 Bert thinks that spare time is as important as school.

## Answers

### Employability dialogue

1 It is stressful. – She works in a kindergarten/nursery. – She works six hours every day. – She works from 9 a.m. till 3 p.m. – Tomorrow will be her last day. **(Any two)**

2 She babysat for her sister. – She looked after the neighbour's kids. **(Either one)**

3 She helps with sport activities. – She helps with lunch. – She sings with the children. – She takes them to the toilet. **(Any three)**

4 It is always very noisy/loud. – You need to check the number of kids regularly. – Every child has (their own) problems (which you must know/be aware of). – You always have to tidy up. – You always have to clean up (toys, shoes, tables). **(Any three)**

5 She wants to work with animals. – She wants to work in a zoo. – She wants to work in an animal refuge. – She wants to be a dog handler/dog trainer. – She wants to be a vet. **(Any two)**

6 Anne thinks her work experience is helpful.

## Answers

### Culture dialogue

1  She can get out of her small town. – She gets to see the wider world. – Berlin is a modern city. – Berlin has many attractions. – Berlin has international flair. **(Any two)**
2  They will stay in a youth hostel. – They will stay in the city centre. – They will have four beds in a room. – They will have a shower facility. – Breakfast will be included. – They will stay near the zoo. **(Any three)**
3

| Day | Morning | Afternoon | Evening |
|---|---|---|---|
| **First Day** | Sightseeing (by bus) | Visit a museum/ take photos (at the Brandenburg Gate) | Restaurant (in Alexanderplatz) |
| **Second Day** | Olympic Stadium | Visit an ice-rink/see (Berlin) ice hockey team in training | Club |
| **Third Day** | Shopping (Eurocenter)/ zoo | Holocaust Memorial visit | Back home |

4  Frank is interested in the trip but has not read the programme.

# Chapter 9

## Answers

### Society

1  60% of 12-year-olds are members of a sport club. – 40% of 18-year-olds are members of a sport club. **(Either one)**
2  You learn (about) honesty. – You learn (about) fairness. – You learn to stick to rules. – You learn (about) solidarity. – You learn (about) partnership. **(Any three)**
3  Festivities for Christmas – Festivities for the New Year – holiday camps in the summer – day trips in the summer – extra training in the summer. **(Any two)**
4  To be tolerant – to solve conflicts – to understand other teenagers and adults – to take responsibility. **(Any three)**
5  Sport clubs offer fitness and opportunities for social learning.

## Answers

### Learning

1 They get a bad grade. – They have to stay behind after school. – Parents will be informed/Arguments at home. **(Any two)**
2 Teachers do not (really) check homework. – Teachers are content when homework has been done/when students have done homework (at all). – You cannot find out whether you answered correctly or not. – It is not unusual for teachers to forget about homework/forget they have set homework. **(Any three)**
3 You need help. – Children whose parents cannot afford a private tutor are disadvantaged. – If both parents work full time, they come home late. – If both parents work full time, they might not have time to help their children with homework. **(Any two)**
4 Teachers cannot correct the homework of 150 students each week. – They would not have time to prepare lessons. – They would have to work around the clock/non-stop. **(Any two)**
5 Sarah wants homework to be meaningful and manageable.

## Answers

### Employability

1 Children love to talk about the future. – Children like to see themselves as adults (in exciting jobs.) **(Either one)**
2 They dream about making pets/animals healthy. – They dream about helping pets/animals in pain. – They dream about cuddling cute pets/animals. **(Any two)**
3 Vets have to deal with nervous/aggressive animals. – Most vets work in agriculture/in a cow shed/in a pig shed/on a chicken farm. – Sometimes a vet must put an animal to sleep. – Vets need strong nerves/ the understanding that they help animals (when they put them to sleep). **(Any three)**
4 People who cannot look at blood. – People who are scared of animals. – People who do not want stress in their job. – People who do not want a long period of training. – People who do not want to work at weekends/in shifts. **(Any three)**
5 Being a vet can be a dream job for the right person.

## Answers

### Culture

1  They have different interests (from their parents). – They want to be independent. – They want to sleep late. – They prefer a tent (to a hotel). **(Any two)**
2  Parents should plan the journey/holiday with their kids. – They should understand the wishes of young people. – They should respect the wishes of young people. – They should invite a friend. **(Any two)**
3  A holiday house – near a town – big/spacious – with a garden – Young people should have their own room/a parent-free zone. – TV – internet access. **(Any three)**
4  Sun, sand and sea – beach parties – water sports (opportunities). **(Any two)**
5  Teenagers and their views should be considered by parents before and during the holiday.

# Chapter 10

## Answers

### Society monologue

1  Caroline has a brother, two sisters, a stepbrother and a stepsister. – They are eight people in the family (altogether). – Caroline has five siblings. **(Any one)**
2  Many people think that six kids make too much noise/are too noisy. – Many people think that a large family is untidy. – They have two dogs. – They need parking for two cars./They have two cars that need a parking space. **(Any two)**
3  The house is in the country. – They house is near Rostock/in the north-east of Germany. – The house is huge/very big/spacious. – Each child has a room of their own. – They have a big garden. **(Any three)**
4  By bus – stepfather takes them. **(Either one)**
5  Caroline loves life in a large family despite some problems.

## Answers

### Society dialogue

1 There are only minor/little problems (when he wants to bring friends home/when he wants to have a party). – There are four TVs in the family. – Everybody has a small netbook so they don't argue about the internet. **(Any two)**
2 a) Mother has/draws up a household plan. – Mother has/There is a family calendar. **(Either one)**
   b) He has to hoover. – He has to feed the dogs. – He has to take the dogs for a walk/walk the dogs. **(Any two)**
3 They need two trolleys in the supermarket. – They have three washing machines. – They have a minibus as their family car. **(Any two)**
4 They can all stay together. – The dogs can come too. – There is lots of space. – They can cook for themselves. – They don't have to spend so much money. **(Any three)**
5 He wants to find a good job. – He wants to travel the world/to Africa and Asia. – He wants a partner (later). – He wants one or two kids (later). **(Any one)**

## Answers

### Learning monologue

1 Learning is fun (for him). – His teachers are patient. – His teachers are never moody. – His teachers understand his interests. **(Any two)**
2 He did not have as much homework (in primary school). – They/ He used to sing a lot (in primary school). – He used to play a lot (in primary school). – He had different teachers (in grammar school). – He had to change classrooms for every lesson. **(Any three)**
3 He will do his Highers this year. – He wants to/would like to go to university. – He wants to/would like to be an engineer. – He will be the first in his family with a university degree. **(Any two)**
4 Andreas thinks that education helps him to achieve his life dreams.

## Answers

### Learning dialogue

1 Mandy took the dog for a walk. – She picked up/collected a parcel from the post office. – Her mother phoned her. – Mandy went to get milk from the supermarket. **(Any two)**
2 She (always) has lots to do for Maths and German/for her main subjects. – She has weekly homework in History/English/Biology. – Sometimes she has no time for her hobbies and friends. **(Any two)**
3 Nancy often goes away at the weekend (with her parents). – Nancy is on tour with her dance club (at the weekends). – Mandy has no time during the week to see Nancy. **(Any two)** ⇨

4  a) Mandy is musical. – It is fun. – She will be able/can play in a concert soon. **(Any two)**
   b) Mandy has her friends there. – She loves athletics. – Most of all she loves sprinting. **(Any one)**
5  (Every Sunday) she does/works out a plan (for the week). – She writes down what she must do. – She writes down when she has to do it (and how long). – She does a lot of her homework on Saturday and Sunday. – She phones her friends if she needs help. – Mandy and her friends do homework together. **(Any three)**

## Answers

### Employability monologue

1  Many students want to work in the summer. – Grammar school students want to work in the summer. – There are not so many supermarkets and shops in his home town. **(Any two)**
2  a) His German teacher gave him tips (for the interview). – His German teacher discussed the questions for the interview/the interview questions. **(Either one)**
   b) His parents went clothes shopping with him./His parents bought him the right clothes for the interview. – They told him what there was to do in a supermarket. – They told him to be friendly/polite. **(Any one)**
3  Markus was a bit nervous. – The staff manager was very friendly. – She showed him the supermarket. – She told him he would stack shelves/clean up/work at the till. – Markus answered all the questions. – Markus thanked her for the interview. **(Any three)**
4  Markus feels that he has been very lucky to get this job.

## Answers

### Employability dialogue

1  The work is too hectic. – Some guests are unfriendly. – The cook was often moody. **(Any two)**
2  She cleaned the tables. – She washed the dishes (in the kitchen). – She served drinks. – She served food. – She helped at the cash register. **(Any three)**
3  They were a good team. – They helped each other. – The boss was difficult. – The boss was in a bad mood. **(Any two)**
4  Most guests were no problem. – Some people could not wait five minutes for a coffee. – The soup was too cold. – The food was too hot. **(Any two)**

⇨

5 She would like to work with animals/in a zoo/in a rescue centre. –
   She is interested in agriculture/in working with horses/in working
   with big animals. **(Any one)**
6 You find out what the right job is. – You find out what you have
   to do in the job. – She thinks all students should do a work
   experience/have a part-time job/work in the holidays. **(Any two)**

## Answers

### Culture monologue

1 Christine and her friends can spend more time together. – They can
   do all the things that teenagers like. **(Either one)**
2 They will stay at a campsite. – It is very modern. – It is directly
   on the beach. – They can learn to surf. – They can play beach
   volleyball. – There is a small supermarket nearby. – There is a small
   golf course nearby. **(Any three)**
3 Rostock has a big university/a university with about 14,000 students. –
   You can do water sports in Rostock. – You can go by ferry (from
   Rostock) to Denmark/Sweden. **(Any two)**
4 Her parents have different interests. – Her parents like to go to a
   museum/a restaurant. – Christine is sporty/wants active holidays.
   **(Any one)**
5 Christine thinks that holidays without parents are a good
   preparation for life.

## Answers

### Culture dialogue

1 They will take the train (Friday afternoon). – They will arrive at
   8 p.m. – They will walk/take a taxi to the hotel. – They will return
   on Monday night. **(Any two)**
2 Stefan booked the hotel online. – Stefan booked the train tickets
   online.
3 a) They will go on a sightseeing tour. – They will visit the Wall
      Museum/a museum. – They will go up the TV tower. **(Any two)**
   b) They will eat in a Mexican restaurant. – They will watch a film (in
      the Sony Center). **(Either one)**
4 His parents are very modern. – His parents are very understanding. –
   They trust him. – His mother thinks one can only be independent if
   one organises something oneself. – His parents know his friends very
   well. **(Any three)**
5 Switzerland.–St Petersburg in Russia **(Either one)**
6 He and his friends have part-time jobs. – They have saved the
   money. – He got money from his grandparents. **(Any one)**

# Chapter 13

## Society

### Activity 1

**Answers**

fleißig – faul; schüchtern – selbstbewusst; lustig – ernst; hilfsbereit – egoistisch; motiviert – unmotiviert

### Activity 2

**Answers**

Meine Familie ist relativ groß, denn wir sind sechs Personen. Ich habe zwei Schwestern, die Susanne und Jessica heißen. Dann habe ich auch noch einen Bruder und einen Stiefbruder – Thomas und Steffen. Bei uns zu Hause ist es nie langweilig, aber manchmal finde ich es ziemlich stressig, weil das Leben in einer großen Familie hektisch sein kann.

Wir verstehen uns gut und haben ein gutes Verhältnis zu einander. Meine Mutter und mein Stiefvater sind moderne Eltern, sie lachen gern und haben viel Verständnis für uns Kinder. Ich liebe meine Familie.

### Activity 3

**Answers**

1 Tom hat eine relativ große Familie.
2 Seine Eltern, seine drei Brüder und er wohnen in einem Bauernhaus auf dem Land.
3 Das Haus ist sehr groß aber auch sehr alt.
4 Jeden Tag hilft Tom im Haushalt.
5 Er geht mit dem Hund spazieren und bringt den Müll raus.
6 In seiner Freizeit spielt er sehr gern Computerspiele und Fußball.
7 Was machst du in deiner Freizeit?

## Activity 4

**Answers**

**Jessica**

| | |
|---|---|
| very important | *super wichtig* |
| a rather small family | *eine relativ kleine Familie* |
| my circle of friends | *mein Freundeskreis* |
| We get on well with each other | *Wir kommen gut miteinander aus* |
| helpful and understanding | *hilfsbereit und verständnisvoll* |

**Thomas**

| | |
|---|---|
| most friends | *die meisten Freunde* |
| together | *zusammen* |
| girlfriend | *Freundin* |
| the prettiest smile in the world | *das hübscheste Lächeln der Welt* |
| moreover | *außerdem* |

**Bernd**

| | |
|---|---|
| more important than | *wichtiger als* |
| four siblings | *vier Geschwister* |
| on a farm | *auf einem Bauernhof* |
| in the country | *auf dem Land* |
| in the household | *im Haushalt* |

**Susi**

| | |
|---|---|
| constantly away | *ständig unterwegs* |
| senior consultant | *Chefarzt* |
| I attend a boarding school | *ich besuche eine Internatsschule* |
| if you want to talk | *wenn man reden möchte* |
| their parents | *ihre Eltern* |

## Activity 5

**Answers**

1  There is no correct or incorrect answer to the first part of the activity as it is up to the candidates whether they would or would not do what the statement says.
2  Possible sentences:
   ● Ich würde mit meinem besten Freund oder meiner besten Freundin darüber reden./Ich würde nicht mit meinem besten Freund oder meiner besten Freundin darüber reden.
   ● Ich würde mit meinen Eltern darüber reden./Ich würde nicht mit meinen Eltern darüber reden.
   ● Ich würde das erste Date auf den Facebook-Status auf die Pinwand posten./Ich würde nicht das erste Date auf den Facebook-Status schreiben.
   ● Ich würde ins Kino gehen und in der letzten Reihe sitzen./Ich würde nicht ins Kino gehen und in der letzten Reihe sitzen. ⇨

⇨
- Ich würde in ein Café in der Stadtmitte gehen./Ich würde nicht in ein Café in der Stadtmitte gehen.
- Ich würde coole Klamotten tragen./Ich würde keine coolen Klamotten tragen.
- Ich würde Aftershave oder Parfüm tragen./Ich würde kein Aftershave oder Parfüm tragen.
- Ich würde den kleinen Bruder oder die kleine Schwester mitnehmen./Ich würde nicht den kleinen Bruder oder die kleine Schwester mitnehmen.
- Ich würde den älteren Bruder oder die ältere Schwester mitnehmen./Ich würde den älteren Bruder oder die ältere Schwester nicht mitnehmen.
- Ich würde das Mobiltelefon zu Hause lassen./Ich würde das Mobiltelefon nicht zu Hause lassen.

## Activity 6

**Answers**

1 Fußball
2 Tennis
3 Schwimmen
4 Golf
5 Fotografieren
6 Lesen
7 ein Instrument spielen
8 Zeichnen
9 im Internet surfen
10 Schach

## Activity 7

**Answers**

1 Man sollte viel Wasser trinken, weil der Körper hydriert sein muss.
2 Meine Mutter isst keine Schokolade, weil Schokolade zu viel Zucker und Fett hat.
3 Mein Vati raucht nicht mehr, weil er gesünder leben will.
4 Jeden Tag esse ich Obst und Gemüse, weil das fast keine Kalorien hat.
5 Drogen sind ein großes Problem für Jugendliche, weil sie süchtig werden können.
6 Alkohol ist die gefährlichste Droge, weil man überall Alkohol kaufen kann.
7 Ich rauche nicht, weil die Klamotten stinken und es zu viel Geld kostet.
8 Meine Schwester joggt jeden Morgen durch den Park, weil sie fit bleiben will.
9 Mein bester Freund hat eine Medaille im Schwimmen gewonnen, weil er immer hart trainiert hat.
10 Nächstes Jahr werde ich einen Halbmarathon laufen, weil ich Geld für ein Kinderkrankenhaus sammeln und spenden will. ⇨

**Translated sentences:**

1  One should drink a lot of water because the body should be hydrated.
2  My mother doesn't eat chocolate because chocolate has too much sugar and fat.
3  My dad doesn't smoke anymore because he wants to live more healthily.
4  Every day I eat fruit and vegetables because they have almost no calories.
5  Drugs are a big problem for young people because they can become addicted.
6  Alcohol is the most dangerous drug because one can buy alcohol everywhere.
7  I don't smoke because my clothes smell and it costs too much money.
8  My sister jogs through the park every morning because she wants to stay fit.
9  My best friend won a medal in swimming because he always trains hard.
10  Next year I am going to run a half-marathon because I want to donate/raise money for a children's hospital.

## Activity 8

### Answers

a)  **das Fernsehen**: ein Kinderprogramm sehen – keinen Lieblingsfilm haben – Seifenopern langweilig finden – Talentshows peinlich finden – einen eigenen Fernseher mit DVD-Spieler haben

   **das Internet**: einen Breitbandanschluss haben – mit Freunden chatten – abends surfen – ab und zu mailen – regelmäßig skypen – ein Facebook-Profil haben

   **das Handy**: einen preiswerten Vertrag haben – eine Twitter-Funktion haben – Fotos machen können – kurze Videos machen können

b)  1  Seit drei Jahren haben wir einen Breitbandanschluss zu Hause.
   2  Jeden Abend sieht meine Oma das Kinderprogramm mit meinem kleinen Bruder.
   3  Am Wochenende chatte ich den ganzen Tag mit meinen Freunden.
   4  Abends surft meine Mutter im Internet.
   5  Ab und zu mailt meine Tante Fotos aus Amerika.
   6  Mit meinen Freunden kann ich regelmäßig in Deutschland skypen.
   7  Endlich haben meine Eltern einen preiswerten Vertrag für Telefon und Internet.
   8  Seit einer Woche hat meine Katze ein Facebook-Profil!
   9  Meiner Meinung nach hat meine Freundin keinen Lieblingsfilm.
   10  Sehr oft findet mein Opa Seifenopern langweilig.
   11  Jedesmal finde ich die Talentshows peinlich.
   12  Mit Sicherheit hat Sabines Handy eine Twitter-Funktion.
   13  Im Urlaub kann ich mit meinem neuen Handy Fotos machen.
   14  Zu Weihnachten möchte mein Bruder einen eigenen Fernseher mit DVD-Spieler haben.
   15  Ohne Probleme kann Thomas mit seiner Kamera kurze Videos machen.

## Activity 9

**Answers**

a) 1 Meine Heimatstadt hat ein Rathaus in der Stadtmitte.
2 In der Stadt gibt es einen Supermarkt neben der Post.
3 Meine Heimatstadt hat eine Schule mit etwa 500 Schülern.
4 Es gibt auch ein Museum und eine Burg.
5 In der Stadt findet man ein Einkaufszentrum mit vielen Geschäften.
6 Es gibt einen Bahnhof und einen Flughafen.
7 Meine Heimatstadt hat eine Schwimmhalle sowie ein Fitnessstudio.
8 Es gibt auch einen Golfplatz und ein Fußballstadion.

b) 1 Meine Heimatstadt hat ein historisches Rathaus in der Stadtmitte.
2 In der Stadt gibt es einen modernen Supermarkt neben der Post.
3 Meine Heimatstadt hat eine sehr gute Schule mit etwa 500 Schülern.
4 Es gibt auch ein interessantes Museum und eine mittelalterliche Burg.
5 In der Stadt finden man ein großes Einkaufszentrum mit vielen Geschäften.
6 Es gibt einen kleinen Bahnhof und einen internationalen Flughafen.
7 Meine Heimatstadt hat eine tolle Schwimmhalle sowie ein preiswertes Fitnessstudio.
8 Es gibt auch einen kleinen Golfplatz und ein traditionelles Fußballstadion.

## Activity 10

**Answers**

1 does not like it – it is too small and boring and there is nothing there for young people
2 does not like it – there is no train station and no university and all young people move away after they finish school
3 likes it – the inhabitants are friendly and helpful
4 likes it – has family and friends there
5 does not like it – wants to move as soon as possible and finds life in a city much more interesting
6 likes it – it is the best town in the world
7 likes it – nowhere is as beautiful/lovely as home

# Learning

## Activity 1

**Answers**

1 c   2 f   3 a   4 i   5 d   6 g   7 e   8 b   9 h   10 j

## Activity 2

**Answers**

1 Ich mag meine Schule, weil die Lehrer Zeit für die Schüler haben.
2 In der Schulkantine kann man etwas Warmes essen, denn die Köchinnen kochen jeden Tag selbst.
3 Wir können Hausaufgaben in der Schule machen, denn wir haben eine Schulbibliothek.
4 Ich finde meine Schule sehr modern, weil es sehr viele Computer gibt.
5 Die Lehrer sparen Papier, weil jedes Klassenzimmer einen Computer und eine elektronische Tafel hat.
6 Ich gehe gern in die Schule, denn ich bin neugierig und lerne gern.
7 Unsere Schule hat einen eigenen Bus, weil wir oft zu Sportwettkämpfen fahren.
8 Die Eltern sind immer sehr gut informiert, denn die Schule hat eine Webseite mit aktuellen Nachrichten.
9 Jüngere Schüler lernen Schwimmen im Sportunterricht, weil unsere Schule einen kleinen Pool hat.
10 Ich gehe gern zur Schule, denn ich habe meine Freunde dort.

## Activity 3

**Answers**

1 Man darf in der Schule nicht rauchen.
2 Man muss püntklich zum Unterricht kommen.
3 Ich kann mein Handy mit zur Schule bringen.
4 Aber ich darf mein Handy im Unterricht nicht benutzen.
5 Wir können die Hausaufgaben in der Schulbibliothek machen.
6 In meiner Schule müssen wir Schuluniform tragen.
7 Wir dürfen im Unterricht zur Toilette gehen – aber wir müssen den Lehrer fragen.
8 Darfst du in der Schule Kaugummi kauen?
9 Wann musst du morgens in der Schule sein?
10 Wo kannst du Mittag essen?

## Activity 4

**Answers**

1 Herr Klein ist langweilig, aber Herr Schnarchmann ist langweiliger.
2 Frau Winter ist freundlich, aber Frau Sonnenschein ist freundlicher.
3 Herr Hoffmann ist cool, aber Herr Ferrari ist cooler.
4 Frau Meisel ist launisch, aber Frau Sauer ist launischer.
5 Herr Kern ist motiviert, aber Herr Aktionsmann ist motivierter.
6 Frau Groß ist hilfsbereit, aber Frau Samariter ist hilfsbereiter.
7 Herr Berg ist musikalisch, aber Herr Singer ist musikalischer.

8  Frau Maus ist kreativ, aber Frau Künstler ist kreativer.
9  Herr Schmidt ist sportlich, aber Herr Renner ist sportlicher.
10  Frau Siemens ist geduldig, aber Frau Zeitner ist geduldiger.

## Activity 5

**Answers**

1  Ich werde mit 16 die Schule verlassen.
2  Meine Schwester wird Medizin in Edinburgh studieren.
3  Wann wirst du das Abitur machen?
4  Später werde ich in einer Großstadt wohnen.
5  Vielleicht werde ich ein Brückenjahr in Deutschland machen.
6  Mein Freund und ich werden eine Weltreise machen.
7  Mein Vater wird im September einen neuen Job bekommen.
8  Meine Eltern und ich werden im Sommer nach Berlin fliegen.
9  Mit 18 Jahren werde ich meine Fahrerlaubnis machen.
10  In der Zukunft werde ich heiraten.

## Activity 6

**Answers**

1 d   2 f   3 j   4 b   5 g   6 i   7 e   8 a   9 h   10 c

## Activity 7

**Answers**

1  Ich fahre mit dem Fahrrad zur Schule.
2  Ich habe meine Schultasche in dem Auto/im Auto vergessen.
3  Thomas sitzt in der Klasse neben mir.
4  Die Hausaufgaben stehen in dem/im Hausaufgabenheft.
5  Meine Klasse kommt gut mit dem Englischlehrer aus.
6  Ich komme nicht gut mit der Chemielehrerin aus.
7  Gestern bin ich in der Sportstunde gefallen – aber ich bin okay.
8  Manchmal habe ich Probleme mit dem Schulessen, denn es
   schmeckt nicht so gut.
9  Viele Schüler kaufen das Mittagessen in einem Café oder in dem/
   im Supermarkt.
10  Meine Schule ist in der Stadtmitte, sodass viele Schüler mit der
    Straßenbahn oder mit dem Zug zur Schule kommen.

## Activity 8

**Answers**

1 Die Schule beginnt um 9 Uhr.
2 Ich fahre jeden Tag mit dem Bus zur Schule./Jeden Tag fahre ich mit dem Bus zur Schule.
3 Es gibt mittwochs einen Sportklub in der Schule.
4 Ich habe am Freitag eine Doppelstunde Mathe – das ist toll!/Am Freitag habe ich eine Doppelstunde Mathe – das ist toll!
5 Wir essen in der Mittagszeit in der Schulkantine./In der Mittagszeit essen wir in der Schulkantine.
6 Ich komme um 16 Uhr nach Hause./Um 16 Uhr komme ich nach Hause.
7 Ich werde nächstes Jahr in der Schule bleiben./Nächstes Jahr werde ich in der Schule bleiben.
8 Ich mache am Wochenende meine Hausaufgaben und besuche meine Freunde./Am Wochenende mache ich meine Hausaufgaben und besuche meine Freunde.
9 Ich lerne für Tests/Klassenarbeiten früh morgens./Früh morgens lerne ich für Tests/Klassenarbeiten.
10 Ich sehe am Nachmittag fern./Am Nachmittag sehe ich fern.

## Activity 9

**Answers**

1 a) Meiner Meinung nach ist Schuluniform altmodisch und lästig.
  b) Ich bin der Meinung, dass Schuluniform altmodisch und lästig ist.
2 a) Meiner Meinung nach verliert man durch Schuluniform seine Individualität.
  b) Ich bin der Meinung, dass man durch Schuluniform seine Individualität verliert.
3 a) Meiner Meinung nach hat man durch Schuluniform ein Team-Gefühl.
  b) Ich bin der Meinung, dass man durch Schuuniorm ein Team-Gefühl hat.
4 a) Meiner Meinung nach ist man bei Klassenfahrten in Schuluniform sicherer.
  b) Ich bin der Meinung, dass man bei Klassenfahrten in Schuluniform sicherer ist.
5 a) Meiner Meinung nach kann Schuluniform manchmal teuer sein.
  b) Ich bin der Meinung, dass Schuluniform manchmal teuer sein kann.
6 a) Meiner Meinung nach sehen alle Schüler mit Schuluniform gleich aus.
  b) Ich bin der Meinung, dass alle Schüler mit Schuluniform gleich aussehen.

⇨

7 a) Meiner Meinung nach verhindert Schuluniform Mobbing in der Schule.

b) Ich bin der Meinung, dass Schuluniform Mobbing in der Schule verhindert.

8 a) Meiner Meinung nach sollte man Markenkleidung nicht in der Schule tragen.

b) Ich bin der Meinung, dass man Markenkleidung nicht in der Schule tragen sollte.

9 a) Meiner Meinung nach kann man in der Freizeit Markenkleidung tragen.

b) Ich bin der Meinung, dass man in der Freizeit Markenkleidung tragen kann.

10 a) Meiner Meinung nach löst Schuluniform das Mobbing-Problem nicht.

b) Ich bin der Meinung, dass Schuluniform das Mobbing-Problem nicht löst.

## Activity 10

**Answers**

|  |  |  |
|---|---------|--------|
| 1 | comprehensive school | *Gesamtschule* |
| 2 | the school day starts | *der Schultag beginnt* |
| 3 | all-day-school | *Ganztagsschule* |
| 4 | a lunch break | *eine Mittagspause* |
| 5 | in the playground | *auf dem Schulhof* |
| 6 | the latest school stories | *die neusten Schulgeschichten* |
| 7 | The teacher can explain very well. | *Die Lehrerin kann toll erklären.* |
| 8 | I am also not interested in | *Ich interessiere mich auch nicht für* |
| 9 | two left hands | *zwei linke Hände* |
| 10 | I am very good at | *Ich bin sehr gut in* |
| 11 | one school trip per year | *eine Klassenfahrt pro Jahr* |
| 12 | like a big family | *wie eine große Familie* |
| 13 | most teachers | *die meisten Lehrer* |
| 14 | foreign languages | *Fremdsprachen* |
| 15 | abroad | *im Ausland* |

# Employability

## Activity 1

**Answers**

1 d   2 f   3 b   4 h   5 g   6 a   7 j   8 i   9 c   10 e

## Activity 2

**Answers**

1 Eine Lehrerin sollte freundlich und geduldig sein.
2 Ein Arzt sollte hilfsbereit und intelligent sein.
3 Ein Kellner sollte schnell und höflich sein.
4 Ein Sozialarbeiter sollte ruhig und interessiert sein.
5 Eine Sekretärin sollte diskret und ordentlich sein.
6 Ein Taxifahrer sollte ausgeglichen und humorvoll sein.
7 Ein Schulleiter sollte streng und fair sein.
8 Eine Reiseleiterin sollte unternehmungslustig sein.
9 Eine Verkäuferin sollte aufmerksam und selbstbewusst sein.
10 Ein Polizist sollte sportlich und klug sein.

## Activity 3

**Answers**

**Torsten**
Ich habe einen Nebenjob in einem Supermarkt am Stadtrand. Dort arbeite ich jeden Samstag von 8 Uhr bis 16 Uhr. Normalerweise fülle ich Regale auf und helfe im Lager, aber manchmal muss ich auch an der Kasse arbeiten oder saubermachen. Der Job ist gut bezahlt – ich verdiene €6 pro Stunde . Man muss immer freundlich und höflich sein, wenn man mit Kunden spricht. Ich arbeite gern im Supermarkt – aber für immer ist das nichts für mich!

**Marina**
Jedes Wochenende arbeite ich an einer kleinen Tankstelle in der Stadtmitte. Samstags arbeite ich sechs Stunden und sonntags sind es nur vier Stunden – zum Glück, denn ich finde den Job total langweilig. Ich mache Kaffee und warme Snacks, verkaufe Zeitungen und helfe in der Waschanlage. Das Gute ist, dass ich ein bisschen Geld verdiene und manchmal Trinkgeld bekomme. Ich spare auf einen modernen Laptop.

## Activity 4

**Answers**

a) 1 b) (ii); 2 d) (v); 3 a) (iv); 4 e) (i); 5 c) (iii); 6 f) (vi).

b) (i)   In my spare time I play tennis and I go swimming. In addition, I often surf the internet and chat with my friends.

(ii)   My name is Anna Tolson and I am 18 years old. I have been living in Edinburgh since I was born. I speak English and I have been learning German in school for six years.

(iii)   In the next five years I would like to work to gain more experience. Then I would like to take on a management position and have more responsibility.

(iv)   I am interested in this job because I have read a lot about the firm on the internet. I think that I am the right person for the job.

(v)   I am good at modern languages and have a talent for communication. I can plan and organise very well. My knowledge of Maths could be a bit better.

(vi)   I don't think I will want to earn less money than I do now. The pay should correspond with (reflect) the (level of) responsibility.

## Activity 5

**Answers**

a) 1  habe
2  bin
3  habe
4  bin
5  hat

b) 1  gearbeitet
2  gefahren
3  geholfen
4  gemacht
5  gegangen

c) 1  habe
2  hat
3  sind
4  haben
5  ist
6  haben
7  sind
8  haben

## Activity 6

**Answers**

1  Meine Freundin und ich arbeiten seit einer Woche in einem großen Supermarkt.

2  Morgens fahren wir mit dem Bus – die Bushaltestelle ist direkt vor meinem Haus.

3  Jeden Tag stellen wir das Obst und Gemüse auf die Regale und manchmal bringen wir den Müll hinter den Supermarkt, wo die Tonnen stehen. ⇨

4 Meine Freundin und ich sparen das Geld für einen Urlaub an der Ostsee, denn wir wollen gern ohne die Eltern Ferien machen.

5 Wenn wir abends aus dem Supermarkt kommen, sind wir oft müde und wollen schnell nach Hause.

## Activity 7

**Answers**

a)
| | | | |
|---|---|---|---|
| 1 | die Polizistin | 6 | die Lehrerin |
| 2 | die Mechanikerin | 7 | die Sekretärin |
| 3 | die Ärztin | 8 | die Verkäuferin |
| 4 | die Taxifahrerin | 9 | die Pilotin |
| 5 | die Kellnerin | 10 | die Schulleiterin |

b)
1 Sabine möchte Tischlerin in einer Holzwerkstatt werden.
2 Bernd möchte Kurier bei einem Paketservice werden.
3 Mandy möchte Sekretärin in einem Autohaus werden.
4 Torsten möchte Servicekraft bei McDonalds werden.
5 Astrid möchte Pilotin bei der Lufthansa werden.
6 Martin möchte Friseur in einem Salon in der Innenstadt werden.
7 Diana möchte Stuntfrau im Filmstudio werden.
8 Peter möchte Kranfahrer auf einer großen Baustelle werden.
9 Claudia möchte Bäuerin mit eigenem Hof werden.
10 Jörg möchte Krimiautor für einen großen Verlag werden.

## Activity 8

**Answers**

1 Britta hat vor, eine Weltreise zu machen.
2 Jens hat vor, einen Mercedes zu fahren.
3 Doris und Maren haben vor, auf einem Kreuzfahrtschiff zu arbeiten.
4 Ich habe vor, Pferde zu züchten.
5 Silke hat vor, auf den Eiffelturm in Paris zu steigen.
6 Kevin hat vor, nach New York zu fliegen.
7 Nicole und Gerd haben vor, eine Familie zu gründen.
8 Steffen hat vor, Profifußballer zu werden.
9 Markus hat vor, in einer Talentshow zu singen.
10 Nancy und Boris haben vor, ein neues Computerspiel zu entwickeln.

## Activity 9

**Answers**

1 Wie heißen Sie?
2 Wo wohnen Sie?
3 Haben Sie Geschwister?
4 Wofür interessieren Sie sich?
5 Was machen Sie in Ihrer Freizeit?

6 Welche Fremdsprachen sprechen Sie?
7 Was sind Ihre Stärken?
8 Haben Sie eine Fahrerlaubnis?
9 Können Sie Golf spielen?
10 Möchten Sie einen Kaffee mit mir trinken?

## Activity 10

**Answers**

| Name | University or apprenticeship | Reasons for their decision |
|---|---|---|
| Anja | university | She is interested in animals and wants to study veterinary medicine. |
| Tom | apprenticeship | He finds studying boring and prefers active work. He also wants to earn money straight away. |
| Svenja | apprenticeship | Studying takes too long. Her father has his own car garage. She has always been interested in cars and motorbikes. It is a family business. |
| Mark | apprenticeship and university | He wants to be an architect so he has to study. But he will first do an apprenticeship (as a builder) to gain practical experience. |

# Culture

## Activity 1

**Answers**

**Ralph:** Meine Familie und ich fahren sehr gern im Winter in die Berge. Dort wohnen wir in einem Chalet und laufen Ski, gehen Snowboard fahren oder Schlittschuh laufen. Der Schnee und die Kälte stören uns nicht – ich liebe Winterferien!
Ralph loves winter holidays in the mountains.

**Sabine:** Meine Eltern und ich fahren am liebsten in den Süden. Jedes Jahr fliegen wir auf eine Insel im Mittelmeer, wo wir in einer Villa direkt am Strand wohnen. Die Sonne scheint, es ist super warm und ich kann jeden Tag im Meer baden oder im Pool schwimmen. Herrlich!
Sabine loves beach holidays/holidays in the sun.

**Andreas:** Ich fahre sehr gern zelten. Jedes Jahr fährt meine Familie mit dem Wohnmobil und einem kleinen Zelt für mich und meinen Bruder an die Ostsee. Wir sind sehr gern in der Natur – und auf dem Campingplatz ist immer etwas los. Dort sind viele andere Jugendliche, sodass wir schnell Freunde finden.
Andreas loves camping/outdoor holidays.

**Vanessa:** Also ich fahre am liebsten übers Wochenende in eine europäische Großstadt, um die Sehenswürdigkeiten zu besuchen und eine andere Kultur und Sprache kennen zu lernen. Im letzten Jahr war ich in London und Madrid, dieses Jahr steht Hamburg auf dem Programm und von dort aus fliege ich dann nach Edinburg. Ich liebe Geschichte, Museen und Ausstellungen. Kultur ist mir sehr wichtig.
Vanessa likes city breaks/culture holidays.

## Activity 2

### Answers

a) 1 b)   2 d)   3 a)   4 e)   5 c)   6 h)
   7 f)   8 i)   9 g)   10 j)

b) Berlin ist die **Hauptstadt** von Deutschland und befindet sich im **Osten** des Landes. In Berlin **leben** etwa 3,4 **Millionen** Menschen; das **Symbol** der Stadt ist der Berliner **Bär**. Berlin liegt am **Fluss** Spree.

Berlin hat viele **interessante** Sehenswürdigkeiten. Im **Osten** der Stadt ist der Alexanderplatz mit der Weltzeituhr und dem **Fernsehturm**, der 365 Meter hoch ist. Die breite Straße Unter-den-Linden führt durch das **Brandenburger** Tor in den Westen der Stadt. In der Nähe ist der **Reichstag**, das Parlamentsgebäude Deutschlands.

Die größte Einkaufsstraße Berlins heißt **Kurfürstendamm** – die Berliner sagen auch „Ku'damm". Dort gibt es viele Geschäfte und das **Europacenter** mit Restaurants und Souvenirläden.

Berlin hat einen Zoo im Westen der Stadt und einen **Tierpark** im Osten. Es gibt auch viele Theater und **Kabaretts**.

Jedes Jahr kommen viele **Touristen** nach Berlin. Sie besuchen die **Museen** und Kirchen und machen eine **Bootsfahrt** auf der Spree.

## Activity 3

### Answers

1  Baden Württemberg liegt im Süden von Deutschland.
2  Dort wohnen etwa 10,7 Millionen Menschen.
3  Die Hauptstadt des Bundeslandes heißt Stuttgart.
4  Stuttgart ist bekannt für Autoproduktion und Fußball.
5  Im Schwarzwald gibt es Wälder, Seen und Berge.
6  Die Kuckucksuhr ist ein beliebtes Souvenir.
7  Es gibt die Schwarzwälder Kirschtorte und den Schwarzwälder Schinken.

## Activity 4

### Answers

a) 1 Edinburgh; 2 Edinburgh; 3 Glasgow; 4 Glasgow and Edinburgh; 5 Edinburgh; 6 Glasgow; 7 Edinburgh; 8 Edinburgh; 9 Glasgow; 10 Glasgow.

b) 1  Wenn es regnet, kann man mit der U-Bahn fahren.
   2  Wenn es regnet, kann man zum Straßenmarkt Barras gehen.
   3  Wenn es regnet, kann man Galerien und Museen besuchen.
   4  Wenn es regnet, kann man in einem Restaurant oder in einer Kneipe essen gehen.
   5  Wenn es regnet, kann man das nationale Fußballmuseum im Hampden Park besuchen.
   6  Wenn es regnet, kann man mit dem Zug nach Edinburgh fahren.
   7  Wenn es regnet, kann man ins St Enoch Zentrum gehen.   ⇨

8 Wenn es regnet, kann man einen Bummel in der Buchanan Street machen.

9 Wenn es regnet, kann man im Bett bleiben.

## Activity 5

**Answers**

1 a) Meine Eltern und ich **haben** in einem Hotel in der Stadtmitte **gewohnt**.

b) Meine Eltern und ich **werden** in einem Hotel in der Stadtmitte **wohnen**.

2 a) Mein Vater **hat** eine Hafenrundfahrt mit einem kleinen Schiff **gemacht**.

b) Mein Vater **wird** eine Hafenrundfahrt mit einem kleinen Schiff **machen**.

3 a) Meine Mutter und ich **haben** das Miniaturmuseum in der Speicherstadt **besucht**.

b) Meine Mutter und ich **werden** das Miniaturmuseum in der Speicherstadt **besuchen**.

4 a) An einem Abend **haben** wir das Musical „Tarzan" **gesehen**.

b) An einem Abend **werden** wir das Musical „Tarzan" **sehen**.

5 a) Ich **habe** für meine Freunde T-Shirts in Hamburg **gekauft.**

b) Ich **werde** für meine Freunde T-Shirts in Hamburg **kaufen**.

## Activity 6

**Answers**

1 a) Wenn ich genug Geld gespart **habe**, **fahre** ich nach London.

b) Ich **fahre** nach London, wenn ich genug Geld gespart **habe**.

2 a) Wenn meine Eltern Urlaub **haben**, **fliegen** sie nach Amerika.

b) Sie **fliegen** nach Amerika, wenn meine Eltern Urlaub **haben**.

3 a) Wenn meine Klasse nach Berlin **fährt**, **machen** wir eine Stadtrundfahrt.

b) Wir **machen** eine Stadtrundfahrt, wenn meine Klasse nach Berlin **fährt**.

4 a) Wenn mein Austauschpartner nach Schottland **kommt**, **fahre** ich mit ihm zum Loch Ness.

b) Ich **fahre** mit ihm zum Loch Ness, wenn mein Austauschpartner nach Schottland **kommt**.

5 a) Wenn ich Deutschland **besuche**, **möchte** ich München und die Alpen sehen.

b) Ich **möchte** München und die Alpen sehen, wenn ich Deutschland **besuche**.

## Activity 7

**Answers**

| | | | |
|---|---|---|---|
| 1 | Wo | 5 | Wie |
| 2 | Wie lange | 6 | Wer |
| 3 | Wo | 7 | Warum |
| 4 | Was | | |

## Activity 8

**Answers**

1  Wir fahren/reisen in zwei Wochen nach Dresden. In zwei Wochen fahren/reisen wir nach Dresden.
2  Ich buche diese Woche die Flüge im Internet. Diese Woche buche ich die Flüge im Internet.
3  Mein Freund kauft am Wochenende ein Buch über Dresden im Buchladen. Am Wochenende kauft mein Freund ein Buch über Dresden im Buchladen.
4  Meine Eltern tauschen morgen Euros in der Bank. Morgen tauschen meine Eltern Euros in der Bank.
5  Meine Oma/Großmutter backt nächste Woche Kekse für die Reise. Nächste Woche backt meine Oma/Großmutter Kekse für die Reise.

## Activity 9

**Answers**

| | | |
|---|---|---|
| 1 | especially important | *besonders wichtig* |
| 2 | family festivity at the end of the year | *Fest der Familie am Jahresende* |
| 3 | a big Christmas dinner | *ein großes Weihnachtsessen* |
| 4 | The shops are closed. | *Die Geschäfte sind geschlossen.* |
| 5 | in spring | *im Frühling* |
| 6 | on Easter Sunday | *am Ostersonntag* |
| 7 | the Easter bunny | *der Osterhase* |
| 8 | new traditions | *neue Traditionen* |
| 9 | trick or treat | *Süßes oder Saures* |
| 10 | in third place | *an dritter Stelle* |
| 11 | movies | *Kinofilme* |
| 12 | a result of globalisation | *ein Resultat der Globalisierung* |

## Activity 10

**Answers**

1 d)   2 a)   3 c)   4 k)   5 f)   6 g)
7 e)   8 b)   9 l)   10 j)   11 h)   12 i)